BABBLE

BABBLE

CHARLES SAATCHI

Booth-Clibborn Editions

CONTENTS

Marie-Antoinette de Lorraine-Habsbourg, Queen of France, and her children, 1787, Louise Elisabeth Vigée-Le Brun

CHILD ABUSE? GUILTY ON ALL COUNTS.

Although I grew up in the security of a devoted family it never occurred to my parents, and others of their generation, to try and find ways to keep the children amused and entertained at all times – organizing sleep-overs, tickets for the cinema and theatre, and presents being handed over on a weekly basis.

Today's parents feel so guilty about spending too little time with their offspring, or not sticking by all the Principles of Perfect Parenting, we have created children who have been pandered to, catered for, to the point where their futures must hold much disappointment.

Instead of gifts at Christmas and Birthdays, weekly presents remove the excitement of anticipation, or the sense of receiving a real treat. Treats are now two-a-penny. Instead of Children's Hour on the BBC to look forward to, there are now Multiple TV Channels, DVDs, Facebook, PlayStation, Xbox, Theme Parks, Summer Camps, Winter Camps, iPods, 3G Mobile Phones etc. etc.

Have I spoilt my children to unsustainable levels of satisfaction? Guilty on all charges, m'lud.

But why not spoil them, and thoroughly?

The notion that children shouldn't be provided with every available pleasure at all times, that an excess of gratification creates unrealistic expectation, that the rest of their lives cannot match up – is hard to argue with.

So why bother? A pampered child will be able to look back at a childhood of warmth and pleasure. Even if later years are less delightful by comparison, the first 20 years will have provided them with many pleasing memories.

Most children are able to work out that your efforts are simply a means of trying to buy their love, put you down as an easy mark whom they can readily take advantage of, until something better or more enticing turns up.

The most invaluable insight into nice behaviour we have been able to pass on to our progeny went something like this: 'It is better to be charmed than to charm.' By this we meant that what makes people feel good about themselves is feeling as if they have been charming, interesting; in short, have been listened to.

The notion that one should oneself be riveting or aim to be quite the most fascinating person in the room is a vulgarity and just sheer, misplaced vanity. Trying to be charming is self-indulgent; allowing oneself to be charmed is simply good manners.

My own parents were very quick with advice.

"Don't say you don't have enough time. You have exactly the same number of hours per day that were given to Michelangelo, Leonardo da Vinci, Albert Einstein, Mother Teresa, Charles Dickens."

Clearly I have never overcome this breeding ground for inadequacy.

"I had the blues because I had no shoes, until upon the street, I met a man who had no feet."

My dad drilled this depressing little homily into me, in the hope of instilling a sense of proportion about my wailing for a transistor radio.

I was so irritated with his sorry tale, I shoplifted a radio from Woolworths.

My dad did also tell me to "Do what you love and love what you're doing, and you'll never work another day in your life", though he kindly saved this homespun wisdom until he had come to accept that I wasn't ever going to amount to much of an academic. They were around before the era of pushy parenting, and taught us that if you needed a helping hand, there was one at the end of your arm.

Also nowadays, parents strain to get their children into posh schools.

One of our children's first schools was so posh, that when a teacher asked the class "who is Mohammed?" a small boy stuck up his hand and quietly answered "our chauffeur".

Children today don't seem to talk in terms of growing-up to be train drivers or nurses, as earlier generations may have. How much nicer to be a child now, believing that you will be indulged and gratified throughout your hedonistic life.

People often wonder what plays the more pivotal role in children's fate, nature or nurture?

Do they mean what would happen to a 2 week old baby, mother a crack whore, father unknown, if it was adopted by a caring, wealthy couple from New York's Upper East Side, and grew up in a magnificent condo, went to top kindergartens and schools, and was offered a place at Harvard, Yale and M.I.T?

Or what would happen in a parallel universe when a wealthy New York couple forgot their baby at a diner while driving through rural Tennessee to admire the local toothless rednecks sitting out on their porches. The baby was seen as a gift from the Almighty by a fervently religious, but slightly retarded local woman, and grew up in her home in a run-down estate, where petty crime and brutality were an everyday occurrence. Little schooling, and working behind the counter in the local hardware store at 15. No offers from Harvard, Yale or M.I.T.

Now you may well be thinking that Environment is a greater influence on how life turns out, than Genetics. And that the crack baby ending up at Harvard proves the point. The well-heeled baby ending up selling claw hammers reinforces the point further.

I wish I could offer a satisfactory resolution to this verbose bit of whimsy, but as always, nobody knows anything much – certainly not about the interaction of genes and environment, or how their variables play out.

Answers on a Post-It please.

A woodcut of an execution by elephant published in the 1868 issue of *Le Tour Du Monde*

YOUR LAST MEAL ON DEATH ROW.

Didn't you always believe that prisoners on Death Row were offered the last meal of their choice on the evening before execution?

So if you perhaps imagined a final banquet of Roast Pheasant, Dauphinoise Potatoes, Haricots Verts, accompanied by a glass or two of Château Latour, or even a shot of tequila – then pardon me. (Or not, in most cases.)

Sadly, for your last meal prior to execution, your budget is $40, and the food must be bought locally.

Prisoners' choices of last meals are sometimes peculiar.

John Wayne Gacy, one of America's most horrifying serial killers, murdered at least 33 young men between 1972 and 1994; he asked for a bucket of Kentucky Fried Chicken, a rather macabre selection as he had worked at KFC for a number of years, and had preyed on many of his victims there.

Timothy McVeigh, the Oklahoma bomber, asked for two bowls of mint ice cream.

Victor Feguer, executed in 1963 in Iowa, requested a single pitted olive.

I have some handy facts for you about prisoners awaiting the death penalty, to bring up in conversation whenever you may wish:

12.7 years is the average length of stay on Death Row prior to execution, and you will be living in a specific Death Row cell measuring 6 × 9 × 9.5ft.

You are in isolation in your cell except for medical reasons, legal, or media interviews, and other approved visits.

You may shower and exercise every 48 hours, but with no contact with any other prisoner.

Death by lethal injection is now considered the most humane way of killing you. However, it is apparently sometimes extremely painful, and some unfortunates have taken over 20 minutes to die, gasping for air and convulsing. Autopsies often show severe chemical burns to the skin.

Execution by elephant was a common method of capital punishment in Asia, particularly in India. Asian elephants were trained and versatile, able both to kill victims immediately by stepping on their heads, or to torture them slowly over a prolonged period.

Employed by royalty, the elephants were used to signify both the ruler's absolute power and his ability to control wild animals. The sight of elephants trampling on captives horrified European travellers, and the practice was suppressed when the British and other nations colonized the region in the 19th century.

I have a number of suggestions for members of the art world who would benefit from being given the elephant treatment as a performance work at MoMA.

There are, of course, many places around the world whose penal institutions are far less appealing than those in the United States:

Gitarama, Rwanda

7,000 men are detained in a prison built for 400 inmates; each man has only half a square yard of space. Prisoners suffer from rotting feet through standing barefoot on the faeces-covered ground, and advanced septicaemia.

Bang Kwang, Thailand

All prisoners are required to wear leg irons for the first three months of their sentences. Death row inmates have their leg irons permanently welded on.

La Sabaneta, Venezuela

Cholera outbreaks have wiped out 700 inmates in recent years, and frequent riots trigger massacres of prisoners.

Camp 22, North Korea

Life at Camp 22 is reputed to be the slowest and most unpleasant death imaginable. Medical experiments are conducted on inmates, including newborn infants.

Tadmor, Syria

Known for its exceptionally harsh conditions, extensive human rights abuse, torture and summary executions. In 1980 there was a massacre of an estimated thousand prisoners.

Drapchi Prison, Tibet

In June 1998 five nuns died in Drapchi, after five weeks of severe maltreatment. The nuns are reported to have committed suicide together by hanging or choking themselves to death in a storeroom within their cell block. All the nuns were close comrades in their twenties who had been imprisoned for peaceful protests. None of them had long periods left to serve.

Diyarbakir Prison, Turkey

This prison is renowned for its institutionalised atrocity. It is notorious for the sexual abuse of its inmates; prisoners have attempted hunger strikes, set themselves on fire in protest of prison conditions, and committed suicide in order to escape the horrors of this facility. Diyarbakir is known to incarcerate children for sentences of life imprisonment.

Petak, Russia

Each prisoner is kept in a small two-man cell for 22½ hours a day, every day. For an hour and a half a day they may stand in a small cage outside. For the first 10 years of a man's sentence he is allowed two visits a year. Half the prisoners have tuberculosis and a number are clinically insane.

Conditions are unspeakably, unimaginably barbarous in the worst of these dungeons where if disease doesn't cripple you, a guard or another inmate likely will.

However, I'm a believer in the American 3-strikes-and-you're-out rule. I don't like the misery that criminals inflict on the innocent, and I really don't care if I sound like Vlad the Impaler or a *Sunday Express* columnist – I want many more, much bigger prisons, to keep horrible people out of circulation. Those furious groups of deranged, baying people you see on the news, banging on the doors of a police van delivering some child murderer to court – I'm on their side.

Though I may not believe in the death penalty, as you know the majority of people in Britain would advocate its return; clearly they believe we should kill people for killing people to show other people that killing other people is wrong.

I'm familiar with all the cogent arguments put forward by the anti-state-murder devotees. But if it's lives you want to save, there are countless numbers around the world living in squalor and disease who are more deserving of your help, and dying in their hundreds every day.

But may I ask a question of you: why do so many 'last meals' on Death Row include Diet Coke?

Note: The head of Vlad the Impaler was preserved in honey. It was sent to Istanbul where the Sultan had it displayed on a stake as visual proof that the Impaler was dead. Estimates of the number of his victims range from 40,000 to 100,000. He earned his sobriquet because impalement was Vlad's preferred method of torture and execution. Woodcuts from the 16th century show Vlad feasting in a forest of stakes and their grisly burdens outside Braşov, while a nearby executioner cuts apart the victims.

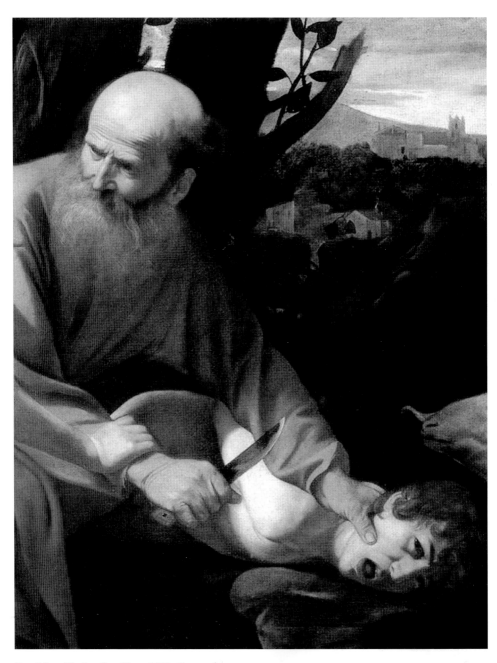

Detail from *The Sacrifice of Isaac*, 1603, Caravaggio

GOD ONLY KNOWS.
HAVE WE FAILED HIM, OR HAS HE FAILED US?

My teenage children do not have a sentimental or even humanitarian view about religion:

God is for the gullible.

"Is God willing to prevent evil, but not able? Then He is not omnipotent.

Is He able, but not willing? Then He is malevolent.

Is He both able and willing? Then from whence cometh evil?

Is He neither able nor willing? Then why call Him God?"

They appear to have wholly embraced these thoughts of Epicurus, written 300 years before the birth of Christ.

For them, it is only the naïve, the misguided who turn to God; He ranks alongside Santa and the Tooth Fairy as likely to be able to grant your wishes.

Do you pray to God in the hope of having your wishes come to pass? I always assumed God would have his own agenda for suddenly offering to make my prayers come true, and I don't care to find out what that agenda may be. Sorry, but I can't see God as a genial Father Christmas type, with rosy round cheeks and twinkly eyes.

I did grow up believing that Abraham was the epitome of a biblical hero. He was the fellow who was ready to sacrifice his son to demonstrate his belief in God. Now, if I told you there was this chap who thought he heard God's voice in his head, chatting to him, asking him to stab his son as a sign of his religious devotion, you would want Social Services to have him sectioned and straitjacketed immediately.

The atheist's strongest card is the perennial question about why bad things happen to good people.

Perhaps it's because our very busy God has better things to worry about than Fair Play and Justice. Or perhaps He finds good people insufferably smug and self-satisfied; that's why horrible men invariably attract the best women. Or maybe He knows that good people will have a fabulous time of it in the next life. And look at those that God gives money to. With enough cash in their pocket the most unpleasant people are considered wise, they are beautiful, and they can sing as well.

Since we were about 10 years old, most of us have wrestled with a vexing concern about whether God actually exists. Personally, I hope He doesn't as I don't think I would like Him very much, have blasphemed frequently, always thought Him arrogant and overbearing, with a misguided perception of righteousness, an insatiable desire for adulation, and profoundly controlling.

My hard-line teenagers also believe the world's worst human invention is religion. The succour and guidance it has bestowed is far too high a price to defray the remorseless horror and bloodshed generated by religious conflict throughout history. For them, mankind's greatest invention has been football, and perhaps, medicine.

And yet, 85% of all weddings are held in religious ceremonies – an eye-opener to people like me, too unbelieving to even be lapsed.

When you visit the World's Great Places of Worship, like Chartres cathedral, they do the job of inspiring shock and awe at the omnipotence of religion. They are equally powerful expressions of the humbleness of the individual in the presence of the Almighty, and it's easy to see how holy devotion has held such sway for so long.

But even the most God-fearing among us must admit that theological fanatics can give anyone pause.

In 1970 Amar Mahant of New Delhi left his job, family and friends to dedicate himself to his spiritual beliefs. In 1973 the clerk raised his right arm aloft in honour of the Hindu deity Shiva – and hasn't put it down for the last 39 years.

Amar's followers claim his sacrifice is a beacon of peace, while other observers believe he has given up the use of his limb to separate himself from the pleasures of mortal life. Amar's suffering has turned his arm into a stump of flesh and bone, with a gnarled, withered hand, and long unclipped fingernails hanging from the end.

He explains that he suffered years of excruciating pain in order to follow his beliefs, but the agony has passed, and his arm has now atrophied into its position after years of non-use.

Devotees of certain religions will undergo astonishing acts of self-sacrifice, sometimes involving starvation or vows of silence. But has Amar's fanatic devotion done any harm to others? Sadly, yes. Many of his acolytes have followed suit, raising their arms for years, even decades.

How can anyone resist the thrill of hearing the views of L. Ron Hubbard, founder of the Church of Scientology? He tells of Xenu, the dictator of the "Galactic Confederacy" who 75 million years ago brought thousands of his people to Earth in spacecraft. Strangely, he then placed them all around volcanoes, and killed them using hydrogen bombs.

Official Scientology teachings hold that the essences of many victims remained, and their spirits form around people to this day, causing them spiritual harm.

The Xenu theory is part of the church's secret "Advance Technology" considered a sacred and esoteric higher plateau, normally only revealed to members who have contributed large amounts of money, and have reached the state of Clear.

The church has gone to considerable efforts to maintain the story's confidentiality, including legal action on the grounds of both copyright and trade secrecy. Despite this, much material on Xenu has leaked to the public via court documents.

Analysts continue to study and dissect Hubbard's writings, and are still intrigued by Xenu, who was apparently about to be deposed from power, and devised a plot to eliminate the recalcitrant population from his dominions. He paralysed, and froze them in a mixture of alcohol and glycol to capture their souls, shipping them off to Earth to be exterminated.

You would be surprised by the many thousands of apparently intelligent members of society who accept this as fact, and see their fellow Scientologists as pioneers, coming to terms with our planet's past, and its impact on life today.

All things considered, I believe God must be very disappointed in his handiwork. Mankind has clearly failed to evolve much in all these years; we're still as cretinous and barbaric as we were centuries ago, and poor God must spend all day shaking His head at our vileness and general ineptitude. Or perhaps, we may just give Him a good laugh. Of course, I hope God likes our art enough to forgive us our sins, particularly mine.

I thought that as I grew more elderly, I would fear His displeasure drawing ever nearer, and the consequences our Lord planned. But having burnt so many bridges getting here, it's a little late to be looking for fire extinguishers.

Note: Paul Haggis, the writer and director of *Crash, The Next Three Days and The Valley of Elah*, and the writer of the screenplay of *Million Dollar Baby*, and Bond films *Casino Royale* and *Quantum of Solace*, left the Church of Scientology after 35 years. He protested and resigned after a staff member at Scientology's San Diego church signed its name to an online petition supporting Proposition 8, which asserted that the State of California should sanction marriage only "between a man and a woman."

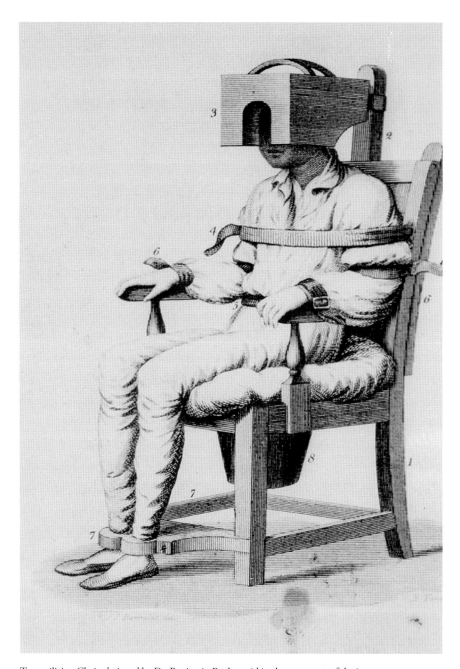

Tranquilizing Chair, designed by Dr. Benjamin Rush to aid in the treatment of the insane

HOW NUTS IS YOUR SHRINK?

If, like me, you have many reasons to be less than secure and self-assured, and like me, and you are far from stable even on your best days, don't for a moment imagine a psychotherapist will be of more help than a physiotherapist.

I have never fully recovered from reading this dissertation delivered in 1992 by Richard P. Bentall, Professor of Clinical Psychology, who is the recipient of awards from the British Psychological Society.

"It is proposed that happiness be classified as a psychiatric disorder and be included in future editions of the major diagnostic manuals under the new name: major affective disorder, pleasant type.

In review of the relevant literature it is shown that happiness is statistically abnormal, consists of a discrete cluster of symptoms, is associated with a range of cognitive abnormalities, and probably reflects the abnormal functioning of the central nervous system.

One possible objection of this proposal remains – that happiness is not negatively valued. However, this objection is dismissed as scientifically irrelevant."

I defy anyone to be stable, secure and self-assured after a few years of this kind of shrink think.

An ex-wife insisted I visited a psychiatrist in an effort to improve me as a hubby. I walked into his house, he looking rather like Leo Sayer, and I could see his eyes light up. Glancing around at his art collection of Hirsts, Emins and other popular favourites, I realized that perhaps he was looking forward to this session rather more than I was.

Anyway, not wanting to disappoint, I made up a twisted tale of increasing weirdness about my need to wear my mother's clothes at night, being too frightened to go inside a chemist's shop, nightmares about squirrels etc.

Eyes glistening, he lapped up every detail of my little problems and booked me in for multiple appointments. But I had bored myself at the end of session one, couldn't face another, and gave up the chase to make more of a fist of my life.

Did you have an imaginary friend when you were a child?

Mine's still around. He hasn't aged. He is still hyper-critical of everything I do, as paranoid as ever, still controlling and dismissive and with the same self-righteous, overbearing attitude. His voice is in my head at all times, scolding my every error, ungracious and belittling about any minor success I may occasionally have.

Anyway that's another tidbit I told my psychiatrist, at our only meeting, in order to make our session more interesting and memorable for him.

He has since written a much-admired paper for *The Lancet* medical journal, describing my problem, where I am referred to as Patient 27. Did I mention my imaginary friend is Caligula?

I also added that his intrusions used to keep me up at night. I'm sure your psychiatrist would probably advise you that sleep disorders are usually a symptom of troubling unresolved problems.

I now sleep the untroubled sleep of the innocent. This involves a variety of medications ranging from Temazepam, Mogadon, Zimovane or Stilnoct, which I mix around so my poor brain doesn't develop immunity to any one of these delightful capsule coshes.

People tell me they have depressing after-effects, leaving you groggy and grumpy the next day, but obviously I wouldn't notice.

Last year my doctor broke the news to me that Temazepam was now to be classified as a Class A drug by the Home Office. He said the only way he could go on prescribing it would require me to become a registered drug addict.

This didn't bother me particularly until he advised me that the Home Office is fabulously leaky and that my spiral-into-drugs-hell would be instantly placed with the *Daily Mail.*

Did you know that you can get immediate advice from a psychiatrist on a number of internet sites including www.here-to-listen.com?

I read about creating a Psychiatric Hotline, with a helpful automated message.

If you are obsessive-compulsive, please press 1 repeatedly.

If you are co-dependent, please ask someone to press 2.

If you have multiple personalities, please press 3, 4, 5 and 6.

If you are paranoid-delusional, we know who you are and what you want. Just stay on the line until we trace the call.

If you are schizophrenic, listen carefully and a little voice inside will tell you which number to press.

If you are clinically despondent, it doesn't matter what number you press. No one will answer.

If you are hallucinatory, please be aware that the object you are holding onto the side of your head is alive and about to bite off your ear.

I can offer two instant cures for you to never require seeing your shrink again: A) Accept that depression is merely anger without enthusiasm. B) Remember psychiatrists don't suffer from insanity. They enjoy every minute of it.

Note: It is simply an urban myth that psychiatrists are more prone to suicide than the rest of us. It may indeed be the case that medical professionals in general have a suicide rate nearly 100% above average. But dentists have a more elevated propensity to take their own lives than psychiatrists and physicians in general. Apparently they feel under-appreciated because nobody likes seeing them.

A nickelodeon cinema in Toronto, Canada, 1910

MY LOVE AFFAIR WITH ORSON WELLES.

How do you handle failure? I handle failure very badly. Bitterly. Indignantly. Girly tears.

I once saw a three-hour BBC interview with Orson Welles, and if it is possible to fall for a man just from seeing him on the telly, Mr Welles has had me as his love slave since.

Welles had manifold reasons to be bitter about life's setbacks, not the least being that his unquestioned prowess as a film-maker didn't stop Hollywood treating him like a disease.

After years of having to panhandle for backing to fund his film projects – all unwanted by the studios, all later to be recognised as exquisite jewels – he eventually had to rely on appearing in TV commercials, endorsing wines or Spanish sherry, to finance his final movies.

Throughout the interview Welles was witty, fascinating, self-deprecating, animated, radiant, sparkling. Without a sullen or bitter bone in his immense body, he was a twinkly-eyed, beguilingly charming giant, not even fractionally undone by the burden of many setbacks and humiliations.

The movie business is more than capable of driving anyone quite insane – the more insane, the more strangely gifted you may be. The story of Orson Welles illustrates vividly that it requires a resolutely secure person to take failure gracefully. Not a hope for most of us, and certainly not me.

A quick glance at the history of Oscar winners and nominations throws up many outstanding films that were passed over as Oscar finalists, with more mundane products regularly picking up the plaudits.

Since 1950, none of the following movies have even been nominated for best film:

North by Northwest

The African Queen

Paths of Glory

Spartacus

Hud

What's Up Doc?

The Manchurian Candidate

The Big Country

Scarface

Vertigo

Kill Bill

Parenthood

Reversal of Fortune

Harold and Maude

Being There

Whatever Happened to Baby Jane?

Lost in America

Minority Report

Jurassic Park

Close Encounters of the Third Kind

Heat

Once Upon a Time in America

Seven

The Searchers

Psycho

Rear Window

The Producers

Toy Story

Some Like It Hot

2001: A Space Odyssey

Lolita

The Shining

Touch of Evil

Gran Torino

Beetlejuice

Edward Scissorhands

Raising Arizona

Advise and Consent

Mean Streets

King of Comedy

Reservoir Dogs

Manhattan

Crimes and Misdemeanors

Broadway Danny Rose

Klute

This is Spinal Tap

Princess Bride

Misery

When Harry Met Sally

Sleepless in Seattle

Bad Day at Black Rock

Sweet Smell of Success

An Officer and a Gentleman

Night of the Hunter

Planes, Trains and Automobiles

Badlands

Three Kings

Airplane!

Blade Runner

Cool Hand Luke

Diner

True Grit

The Usual Suspects

Alien

Hannibal

American Gangster

The Court Jester

Monster

Clueless

The Odd Couple

Barefoot in the Park

The Young Lions

Winchester '73

The Man From Laramie

Hombre

The Day of the Jackal

Cape Fear

Serpico

Changeling

East of Eden

Mrs Doubtfire

To Catch a Thief

Strangers on a Train

A History of Violence

Groundhog Day

The Leopard

Stand by Me

Body Heat

Don't Look Now

Easy Rider

Rio Bravo

Thelma & Louise

Point Blank

Days of Heaven

Papillon

Presumed Innocent

Run Silent Run Deep

Seven Days in May

Imitation of Life

Miller's Crossing

Charlie Wilson's War

The Untouchables

The Asphalt Jungle

Full Metal Jacket

Suddenly, Last Summer

Straw Dogs

Who Framed Roger Rabbit

Compulsion

The Spy Who Came in from the Cold

Lonely Are The Brave

The Long Goodbye

The Wild One

(It isn't only since 1950 that the Oscars have overlooked films of note. In previous years, *Modern Times, City Lights, Duck Soup, Bringing Up Baby, Gilda, A Night At The Opera, His Girl Friday, To Have And Have Not, Kind Hearts And Coronets, Out Of The Past, My Darling Clementine, King Kong, The Life And Death Of Colonel Blimp, The Women* etc. etc. were not included for nomination as Best Film.)

Of course, you may not agree that some of these movies are particularly distinguished. Nonetheless, a list of the nominations for

Oscars over the past 60 years would make the most stoic of men weep. Mr Welles was beaten to an Oscar for *Citizen Kane* in 1942 by *How Green Was My Valley*. But it would be cruel punishment indeed to the Oscar ceremony, which gives us such queasy delight each year, to dwell on the number of times a certifiable dud like *The Greatest Show on Earth* beat a masterpiece like *High Noon* to best picture.

Sadly, in the movies as in life, being the best you can be isn't necessarily a winning formula. Years ago, we bought a large US research company, whose specialist area was working for seven of the eight big Hollywood studios, pre-testing their films. The gentleman running this business was considered an all-powerful guru among the movie community, and his company would screen your movie at a preview stage, and have the audience score it before leaving the theatre. They would tick: a) enjoyed thoroughly; b) quite entertained; c) rather bored, etc; and also a) would see again; b) would recommend; c) would advise against, etc.

They would get ratings for each actor, and often try out different endings, to see which performances could be cut, and which finale worked more favourably. The studios could then determine which movies would be worth supporting heavily with a big marketing budget, and which to quietly give up on.

I thought that it would be illuminating to meet our guru running this company, and find out a little about how all the testing works. The thrust of my question to him was: if all of the studios produce 20 movies a year, but only three of them make substantial profits, five of them do OK, and the others are financial flops, what useful guidelines did his research provide? Three out of 20 hits didn't appear to be a glittering track record for the benefits of pre-testing.

He explained one thing very clearly. "Each multiplex has screens allocated to each studio. The screens need filling. Studios have to create product to fill their screen, and the amount of good product is limited. So you have to go on creating films even if there is only mild enthusiasm for the project, in order to protect your multiplex screen allocation moving over to a competitor studio."

It would be indiscreet for me to pass on other revelations he gave me about the dismal strike rate that Hollywood achieves. But at least I now knew the answer to a question that had often puzzled me – how did that film ever get made?

Detail from *Mr. Pitt Addressing The House Of Commons In 1793*, by Carl Anton Hickel, engraving, 1885

POLITICIANS ARE NOT HYPOCRITES.

If only they were. Hypocrisy would mean they understood truthfulness, or even considered the possibility of sincerity. Before you can be a hypocrite, first you must have genuine beliefs that you can betray.

Ever since our agency created 'Labour isn't working' people occasionally enquire how deeply held are my Tory beliefs.

I also, once, threw myself into the Health Department Anti-Smoking campaign, visited emphysema wards, studied pictures of cancerous lungs, and came up with the grisliest copy I could – puffing away happily as I wrote. How sweet of people to think that advertising copy is written from the heart.

Leaders I like are 'conviction' politicians. So even someone like Ken Livingstone commands attention because he is prepared to stand firmly behind his point of view, however disingenuous the approach, however crackpot the cause, however suspect his motivation.

I obviously feel drawn to politicians who hold forthright views, and are man enough to fight for them – even if their name isn't Winston Churchill, but Margaret Thatcher, Golda Meir, Angela Merkel.

In general, politicians always try to avoid giving offence by sitting on it.

The usual breed who are hungry for power seem to feel it's best to say little of consequence, and can barely land a good blow on a bereft incumbent, relying instead on voters' inertia.

The great ally of dozy, third-rate oppositions-in-waiting is the ennui of a jaded public who think "It's Time For A Change".

I am never sure whether having governments enjoy a fixed term of 4 or 5 years is too long or too short.

In essence, politicians are like nappies. They need to be changed often, and pretty much for the same reasons. Nearly all political leaders don't seem to have adequate answers, until they write their memoirs.

Don't you enjoy elections however? The air is full or speeches, and vice versa. The Left think they are where the righteous should be. The Right try so hard to scramble left, the damp middle ground has become an overcrowded swamp.

Together when they see light at the end of the tunnel, they spend as much as possible to build some more tunnel.

And why wait for the recession to implode to begin organizing our national finances more effectively?

When did Noah build his ark? *Before* the flood.

Our problem is, we all grew up to hear that anyone could become President or Prime Minister; and now we believe it.

No one comes closer to capturing the workings of government than Claud Schuster, who since taking office in 1915, served ten different Chancellors during his 29 years as Britain's senior Civil Servant.

His description of the relationship between the Prime Minister and the Cabinet was graphic: 'Like the procreation of eels, it is slippery and mysterious'.

As someone with a particularly small moral compass, demonstrated by the speed I dropped the Health Department anti-smoking campaign the moment we were offered the Benson & Hedges/Silk Cut cigarettes account, I would have made an outstanding Member of Parliament.

With a limited skill base, minimal intelligence, and very little numeracy, I obviously stood an excellent chance of achieving high office and acclaim in politics.

Or perhaps a senior post in the diplomatic service? Diplomacy is simple stuff; it's the art of letting someone have your way. And remembering to say "Good Doggy" whilst looking for a bigger stick.

In politics, as in business, it's easy to identify what turns people into high achievers.

There are two rules for success.

1. Never tell everything you know.

However, whatever political hue you may be, all decent people want the safety net that the public sector provides for the less fortunate.

But help me understand why in a little country like ours, the National Health Service is the third largest employer in the world, after the Red Army in China and the railways in India?

I find it harder still to comprehend how the world's 200 biggest companies manage to contribute 30% of the world's economy, yet do so employing just 1% of the world's workers. Do top international businesses more readily grasp how to manage themselves, than the world's top politicians know how to manage us?

I have no answer, because I couldn't possibly get my head around the logistics. But neither, apparently have successive governments.

Telling someone they are on a seven-month waiting list for a knee operation on a limb that is very painful, the owner of which cannot afford to go private, is the equivalent of saying "Get rich or walk with a stick".

Sorry, but our politicians, decades of them, have created exactly just that kind of caring society.

I have a further political quandary for you to help me with.

Many people argue that it's foolish in times of austerity for countries to keep up Foreign Aid.

Their argument is cogent – isn't it the transfer of money from poor people in rich countries, to rich people in poor countries?

It sounds brutal, but then the world is.

Tragically, I fear that corruption is now of such epidemic proportions that much of your own charitable contributions overseas, or indeed your government's, is never seen by the intended recipients.

Detail from *A Private View at the Royal Academy, 1881*, 1883, William Powell Frith

THE HIDEOUSNESS OF THE ART WORLD.

Being an art buyer these days is comprehensively and indisputably vulgar. It is the sport of the Eurotrashy, Hedge-fundy, Hamptonites; of trendy oligarchs and oiligarchs; and of art dealers with masturbatory levels of self-regard. They were found nestling together in their superyachts in Venice for this year's spectacular art biennale. Venice is now firmly on the calendar of this new art world, alongside St Barts at Christmas and St Tropez in August, in a giddy round of glamour-filled socialising, from one swanky party to another.

Artistic credentials are au courant in the important business of being seen as cultured, elegant and, of course, stupendously rich.

Do any of these people actually enjoy looking at art? Or do they simply enjoy having easily recognised, big-brand name pictures, bought ostentatiously in auction rooms at eye-catching prices, to decorate their several homes, floating and otherwise, in an instant demonstration of drop-dead coolth and wealth. Their pleasure is to be found in having their lovely friends measuring the weight of their baubles, and being awestruck.

It is no surprise, then, that the success of the über art dealers is based upon the mystical power that art now holds over the super-rich. The new collectors, some of whom have become billionaires many times over through their business nous, are reduced to jibbering gratitude by their art dealer or art adviser, who can help them appear refined, tasteful and hip, surrounded by their achingly cool masterpieces.

Not so long ago, I believed that anything that helped broaden interest in current art was to be welcomed; that only an elitist snob would want art to be confined to a worthy group of aficionados. But even a self-serving narcissistic showoff like me finds this new art world too toe-curling for comfort. In the fervour of peacock excess, it's not even considered necessary to waste one's time looking at the works on display. At the world's mega-art blowouts, it's only the pictures that end up as wallflowers.

I don't know very many people in the art world, only socialise with the few I like, and have little time to gnaw my nails with anxiety about any criticism I hear about.

If I stop being on good behaviour for a moment, my dark little secret is that I don't actually believe many people in the art world have much feeling for art and simply cannot tell a good artist from a weak one, until the artist has enjoyed the validation of others – a received pronunciation. For professional curators, selecting specific paintings for an exhibition is a daunting prospect, far too revealing a demonstration of their lack of what we in the trade call "an eye". They prefer to exhibit videos, and those incomprehensible post-conceptual installations and photo-text panels, for the approval of their equally insecure and myopic peers. This "conceptualised" work has been regurgitated remorselessly since the 1960s, over and over and over again.

Few people in contemporary art demonstrate much curiosity. The majority spend their days blathering on, rather than trying to work out why one artist is more interesting than another, or why one picture works and another doesn't.

Art critics mainly see the shows they are assigned to cover by their editors, and have limited interest in looking at much else. Art dealers very rarely see the exhibitions at other dealers' galleries. I've heard that almost all the people crowding around the big art openings barely look at the work on display and are just there to hobnob. Nothing wrong with that, except that none of them ever come back to look at the art – but they will tell everyone, and actually believe, that they have seen the exhibition.

Please don't read my pompous views above as referring to the great majority of gallery shows, where dealers display art they hope someone will want to buy for their home, and new collectors are born every week.

This aspect of the art world fills me with pleasure, whether I love all the art or not.

I am regularly asked if I would buy art if there was no money in it for me. There is no money in it for me. Any profit I make selling art goes back into buying more art. Nice for me, because I can go on finding lots of new work to show off. Nice for those in the art world who view this approach as testimony to my venality, shallowness, malevolence.

Everybody wins.

And it's understandable that every time you make an artist happy by selecting their work, you create 100 people that you've offended – the artists you didn't select.

I take comfort that our shows have received disobliging reviews since our opening exhibition of Warhol, Judd, Twombly and Marden in 1985. I still hold that it would be a black day when everybody likes a show we produce. It would be a pedestrian affair, art establishment compliant, and I would finally know the game was up.

Some of the new heavy-hitter collectors have asked me how you can tell a good Picasso from a bad one, or a good Damien Hirst from a poor one.

I try not to reply too bluntly, but in reality if you can't tell a good Picasso from a weak Picasso, or powerful Hirst from a lazy one, your collecting days are going to provide you limited satisfaction. That is, after all the whole pleasure of choosing your art.

The key is to have very wobbly taste, like me, and enjoy a real beauty of a Picasso, a jewel that would grace any mantelpiece, and have an equally soft spot for his bizarrely painted 'failures', that I often find satisfyingly effortless and confident.

I have also been asked if I would rather own Picasso's *Les Demoiselles d'Avignon* or Pollock's *Number One*, both in New York's Museum of Modern Art. Fortunately, I'm just not that acquisitive about art. So I would only be prepared to chew off one of my hands, for either.

Another frequent query is whether I believe that either America or

Europe has a better group of artists making contemporary art. I don't play Art Olympics. The US, UK and Germany have the best art schools, so not surprisingly, grow the most sophisticated artists.

But I enjoyed throwing myself at Chinese art, Indian art, Middle Eastern art for our opening year of exhibitions, and found enough work that was invigorating. There is always an energetic, but unsubtle claque talking-up Russia, South America, Japan, Wherever, as the next hot ticket, the new investment goldmine, the source of emerging superstars. I'm sure their reasons are completely patriotic and indeed, altruistic.

When I was talking to France's most prominent art collector, we both agreed that contemporary French artists are too romantic in a sentimentally cloying way, too mired in the glories of their past. They have been paralysed with insecurity since the birth of Abstract Expressionism in New York, unable for decades now to create anything sparked by the present day. Contemporary French art, with very, very few exceptions, is as irrelevant as their Johnny Hallyday was to rock music.

People are also curious about which of the contemporary artists who died young – Jean Michel Basquiat, Eva Hesse, Felix Gonzalez-Torres – I think would have achieved long-term greatness.

Without being too callous, some artists achieve iconic status by dying before their work has a chance to dwindle into stale repetition. So Pollock is revered for his masterpieces, and we will never see what he might have produced had he continued making art for another 30 years.

I have never really loved Basquiat's work, even though I was taken down to dealer Anina Nosei's basement where she had this young boy painting away there, telling everyone who'd listen that in young Basquiat she'd found a genius and for only $500 a picture. Silly me, I found it all derivative and decorative, so that shows how much my taste can be trusted.

Note: The most expensive painting ever sold was *The Card Players* by Paul Cézanne. The transaction of $254 million was made by the Royal Family of Qatar to George Embiricos in 2011.

Detail from *Man Proposes, God Disposes*, 1865, Sir Edward Landseer

GREEN WITH VANITY.

It makes nice people feel good about themselves to do their bit for the planet. But it's vanity of a grotesque kind to believe that mankind, and our "carbon footprint" has more impact on the future of earth than Nature, which bends our planet to its will, as it sees fit.

We serve at the pleasure of Nature and are commanded by its whims – a far greater manipulator of our destiny than 10,000 ExxonMobil and their like.

This would all be a harmless fad, except that it is now costing the West trillions of dollars to go "greener", with the blessing of caring souls and the Kyoto Protocol, while much of the world still lives in crushing poverty or simply starves to death.

It's always worth remembering the Golden Rule: whenever you see a newspaper headline saying something like 'Scientists link butter to heart failure' at Farrell University: the university, the scientists, their research study, their laboratories have all been funded by the Margarine Marketing Board.

The great majority of scientists who are Nobel Prize recipients have no belief, and no vested interest in going along with the global warming propaganda. By vested interest, I refer to those other scientists, whose colossal research grants and data funding is provided by organizations whose profits or influence will be greatly enhanced by suitable statistics; evidence for example, of the desperate need to create wildly expensive and pitifully inefficient wind farms across the world, wherever governments are stupid enough to buy them and decorate their countries with them.

Everyone would be more concerned about global warming, but for a few small facts:

1)   The Earth was hotter 1000 years ago. Temperatures were higher in

the Medieval Warm Period than they were in the 1990s. Britain is one degree Celsius cooler than it was at the time of the Domesday Book.

2) If we look at more recent evidence, the hottest decade of the last century was the 1930s, pre-dating global corporations' supposed destruction of our ecosystems.

3) Greenland got its name from the verdant pastures of grain and hay, which have gradually disappeared over the centuries as ice continues to encroach further.

4) 2008 saw the Northern Hemisphere enjoy its greatest snow cover since 1966. Ice is not disappearing. Arctic ice volume is 500,000 sq km greater than this time last year, and the Antarctic sea-ice is at its highest level since 1979. Polar bear numbers are at record levels of 20–25,000. Fifty years ago, they were 8–10,000.

5) Sea levels are not falling, and holes in our atmosphere are not growing. During some decades sea levels drop by 2 cm. During other decades they rise by 2 cm. Similarly the Earth's ozone layer evolves and fluctuates over the centuries.

Ecologists, and just about everybody else, are infuriated by the excessive packaging on most consumer goods these days.

I will admit to wrap rage, or pack rage as it is sometimes called, a common name for the heightened levels of anger and frustration resulting in the inability to open hard-to-remove packaging, particularly some heat-sealed plastic blister packs. Now sometimes, packaging is deliberately manufactured to be difficult to open, so that over-the-counter medicines have tamper resistance. Sometimes it's simply to reduce pilfering from the contents.

In Britain, over 6,000 people receive hospital treatment each year due to injuries from opening food packaging alone. A 2009 study in *Good Medicine* found that nearly 10% of adults were either injured, or had a member of their family who had been injured while opening a Christmas or birthday gift.

It appears I am not alone in my demented fury at some packaging, scissors or screwdriver in hand, frothing at the mouth.

But it's the sheer volume of excess cardboard, plastic, paper that has become a major burden on the modern world.

Trying to make the world a better place is usually the province of those who want to feel good about themselves. Caring people do occasionally improve things, but sadly, History shows that do-gooders often wreak as much havoc as the most malignant minds. So I may be a disappointing person in many ways, but at least I have never fostered grand designs for social engineering, so beloved of concerned types who want to shape the world, and who mostly just mess up people's lives.

Meaning well is not the same as doing good. For example, if you were a local councillor, burning with a desire to save the planet, wouldn't it be better to start by concentrating on having the lifts on the local estate working, and not stinking of urine?

Or ensuring that lightbulbs in corridors and stairwells get renewed occasionally, in an effort to make them less gloomy and menacing?

You would surely like your constituents to be less fearful of walking around the neighbourhood, hoping not to run into gangs of dumbscum, or tread in piles of vomit or hypodermics or broken bottles.

You would hopefully get round to little projects like these before you set about polishing your Green credentials by obliging everybody to separate their rubbish appropriately, under the threat of a £1,000 fine for miscreants.

Of course, much of the rubbish we carefully separate for recycling is dumped en masse in landfills, in amused cynicism I assume. And a number of countries run a lucrative trade in taking on thousands of tons of other nations' garbage, carefully separated by its citizens, and then heaped together in dumps rather than being reprocessed.

Saving the planet is all well and good but if people are really concerned with making the world a better place, a good start would be having less grandiose aims and lofty ambitions. More humdrum perhaps, but truly more useful.

Death-bed of Louis XIV of France

GROWING OLD IS BETTER THAN NOT.

There are some gratifying advantages to becoming elderly. The first, naturally, is that you are still alive. And it is rather a blessing that eyesight weakens with age, so that your shaving mirror doesn't bear witness too sharply each day to your sorry deterioration.

Also, I can vouch for that truism about advancing age making a person more mellow. So I no longer find questions about how it feels going from an advertising whizz-kid to a past-it pensioner faintly rude, but rather refreshing in their directness.

There is also pleasure to be gained from other people's success, an emotion previously alien to me.

Of course it takes me longer to rest these days than it does to get tired. Your back goes out more than you do. Your knees buckle but your belt won't. Everything hurts, and what doesn't hurt, doesn't work.

Thinking about my joints, I remember only ever having one puff of a marijuana cigarette many years ago. I am looking forward to finally being able to embrace mood-enhancing drugs with no guilt.

Heroin is clearly a marvellous product, as it is so widely admired by satisfied customers all around the world. I can't be doing with hypodermics, track marks or the heated spoon paraphernalia, but if heroin could be offered in more convenient capsule or liquid form, and be easily available at Marks & Spencer or Waitrose, that would be a considerable boon.

As my last years are likely to be crippled with arthritis, dementia, emphysema and heaven knows what else, the prospect of idling away my decline in blissful serenity makes a long life sound quite appealing. Alongside a few like-minded friends, I am looking for a large home somewhere to establish our commune for aged would-be smack heads. It will be very wheelchair-friendly, with many kind nurses to maintain and feed us, change channels on our large plasma screens, and keep us permanently euphoric on Tesco own-brand Freebase Delight.

Growing old is a high price to pay for growing up. Rather than wait for senility to revert us back to dribbling infanthood, we could embrace teenage-dom once again, become more self-absorbed, inconsiderate, narcissistic, ungrateful, lethargically sullen and frenetically animated in equal measure, whenever it suits. I could also experiment with the pleasures of ketamine, skunk, crack, MDMA, and perhaps try my hand at glue-sniffing.

You will find me being attended to by St John's Ambulance at the next all night rave, by about 10.30pm. People who have lived life fully are more fully prepared for death; you only fear death if you've feared life, he whimpered as he was wheeled away.

There is a word in German that doesn't translate into an equivalent in English: Torschlusspanik.

Literally it means 'gate-closing panic' and refers to the idea that the older we get the fewer opportunities are open to us. Simply this means:

At age 4   success is… not wetting the bed.
At age 12 success is… having friends.
At age 18 success is… having a driving licence.
At age 35 success is… having money.
At age 55 success is… having money.
At age 75 success is… having a driving licence.
At age 80 success is… having friends.
At age 85 success is… not wetting the bed.

When people ask if it's important to leave a mark on the world, all I can think is that I would prefer not to leave a stain.

We all die, but not all of us live. On your deathbed, when your life flashes before your eyes, it should be worth watching. Wouldn't you rather burn out than fade away? (cue soaring heavy metal guitar solo).

Without wanting to appear morbid, I have a little collection of Famous Last Words; here are my favourites should you care to share this dubious pleasure:

Louis XIV
(1638–1715)
Why are you weeping?
Did you imagine that I was immortal?
To his attendants who were crying.

Salvador Dalí
(1904–1989)
Where is my clock?

Aldous Huxley
(1894–1963)
LSD, 100 micrograms I.M.
To his wife. She obliged and he was injected twice before his death.

Thomas J. Grasso
(d. 1995)
I did not get my Spaghetti–O's, I got spaghetti. I want the press to know this.
Executed by injection, Oklahoma.

Laurence Olivier
(1907–1989)
This isn't Hamlet, you know. It's not meant to go into the bloody ear.
Said this when a nurse, attempting to moisten his lips, mis-aimed.

Lady Nancy Astor
(1879–1964)
Jakie, is it my birthday or am I dying?
Seeing all her children assembled at her bedside.

Joan Crawford
(1905–1977)
Dammit... Don't you dare ask God to help me.
To her housekeeper who began to pray aloud.

P. T. Barnum
(1810–1891)
[American showman]
How were the receipts today at Madison Square Garden?

Marvin Gaye
(1939–1984)
Mother, I'm going to get my things and get out of this house. Father hates me and I'm never coming back.
Moments later, Gaye was fatally shot by his father, Marvin Gaye, Sr.

George Bernard Shaw
(1856–1950)
Dying is easy, comedy is hard.

Wyndham Lewis
(1884–1957)
Mind your own business.
When his nurse asked him about the
state of his bowels on his deathbed.

King George V of the United
Kingdom
(1865–1936)
Bugger Bognor.
His physician had suggested that he relax
at his seaside palace in Bognor Regis.

Joseph Henry Green
(1791–1863)
It's stopped.
Upon checking his own pulse.

Georg Friedrich Wilhelm Hegel
(1770–1831)
Only you have ever understood me.
…And you got it wrong.
To his favourite student.

Oscar Wilde
(1854–1900)
Either this wallpaper goes, or I do.

Terry Alan Kath
(1946–1978)
[Founding member of the rock band
Chicago]
Don't worry, it's not loaded.
Playing with a gun, the single bullet left
in the chamber killed him instantly.

Saki
(1870–1916)
Put that bloody cigarette out.
To a fellow officer while in a trench
during World War One, for fear the
smoke would give away their positions.
He was then shot by a German sniper
who had heard the remark.

Humphrey Bogart
(1899–1957)
I should never have switched from
Scotch to Martinis.

Paul Claudel
(1868–1955)
Doctor, do you think it could have
been the sausage?

John Sedgwick
(1813–1864)
Nonsense, they couldn't hit an
elephant at this distance.
In response to a suggestion that he
should not show himself over the
parapet during the Battle of the
Wilderness.

Vic Morrow
(1929–1982)
I should have asked for a stunt double.
Morrow said this before filming a
challenging scene for 'Twilight Zone:
The Movie' with a helicopter which
lost control.

Voltaire
(1694–1778)
This is no time to make new
enemies.
*When asked on his deathbed to
forswear Satan.*

James W. Rodgers
(1910–1960)
Why yes, a bulletproof vest.
*On his final request before the
firing squad.*

Given the choice, I would wish to live to 150, every inch of my body functioning in perfect condition, with a nice group of vibrant new friends for whenever my present ones get clapped-out as I stride through my 90s, and I would like to be widely adored by many great-great-grandchildren.

But I have an answer for people who are curious about what happens to us after death. We get buried. Or cremated.

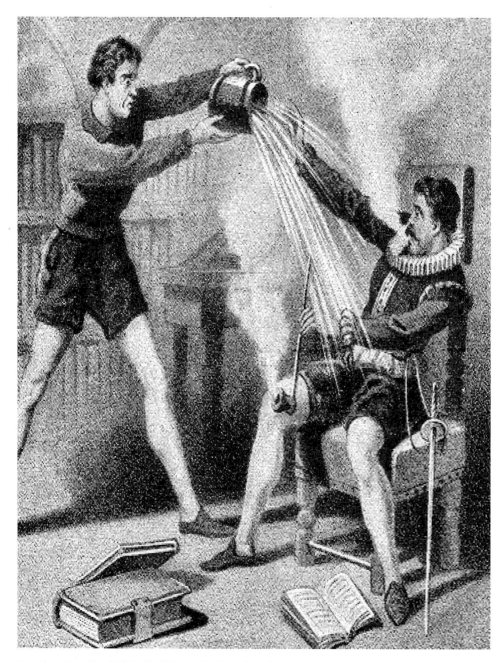

An early anti-smoking lobbyist (Sir Walter Raleigh's smoking alarms his manservant)

SMOKING IS A DYING ART.

I do my bit to support it.

I remember having to write out 500 lines, when caught smoking at school, "Nicotine is an awful curse, it strains the heart and drains the purse." Perhaps that hardened my resolve to enjoy every puff even more fully.

Following the success of the secondary-smoke propaganda, the United States banned smoking from public spaces, including parks in some cities.

Americans then increasingly turned to prescription and over-the-counter pills to help them feel calm and reduce tension, to help them feel cheery and alleviate depression.

It is surely a coincidence that when cigarette lighters became redundant, the spark went out of America; instead of being quick-thinking, fast-talking and confident, Americans grew hesitant and apprehensive, as medicated drug use became overwhelming.

As with everything that happens in America, Britain gamely gets around to it a little later. Buy shares today in UK pharmaceutical companies with leading products on the go-to list that doctors and the NHS prescribe from. The smarter tobacco companies are heavily invested in just these organizations, neatly picking up consumers who smoke, and those who have given up and now require medical mood intervention.

It must confound the anti-smoking brigade that teenagers today are smoking with abandon, perhaps as a result of those graphic warnings placed on cigarette packets, that make smoking more edgy and desirable to our offspring.

Secondary-smoking is a myth that is backed by absolutely no medical evidence. It is a fiction created by the ban cigarettes lobby, who funded a flimsy research study to assist their cause; let's get smoking prohibited in public places like restaurants, offices, bars.

People may not like a smoky atmosphere, and in that sense it would be fair enough to have establishments and offices choose areas for smokers and non-smokers.

But the secondary-smoke argument was so compelling it enhanced demands for a smoking clampdown – under the pretext of protecting workers in pubs and restaurants who may be at risk; a fine argument unless you are aware that the risk is non-existent.

It has been better demonstrated that there is no more health risk in sharing a room with smokers, than there is to walk down a street surrounded by bus and lorry exhausts. Transport fumes, or private car use, will be next on the list of worthy tasks for the Health & Safety interests to get their teeth into, in another well-funded quango.

China, of course, may have a few humanitarian flaws in its government's excesses, but at least their population is free to smoke, and in fact they consume one third of the world's cigarettes, and sales are growing, shareholders in the tobacco industry will be proud to know.

Even a hardened Marlboro spokesperson couldn't argue that cigarette smoking is not a health hazard. But they would claim that many very heavy smokers live to a splendidly old age, with no ill-effects.

Although the links to cancer and heart disease are irrefutable, they would further point out that cigarettes may benefit people in the way smokers have always recited – 'they calm the nerves'.

Doctors who know full well the dangers associated with smoking continue to light up – they take the view that smoking makes life more relaxing and pleasant, and that even if the medical advantages this promotes may be tenuous, they nonetheless exist.

Having seen the arguments from both sides, dedicated to producing trenchant propaganda for the Health Department anti-smoking campaigns, and then cynically working with equal enthusiasm to promote leading tobacco brands, it comes down to this: I enjoy cigarettes greatly, and in great numbers, and I don't believe that 'passive smoking' is harmful to others.

How many times have I tried to give up smoking? Never given it a thought, he wheezed.

In truth I like living, and my aim is to beat the record currently held by Adwaita, 1750 – 2006, a giant tortoise, who was a gift to General Clive of India, from seafarers who found him in the Seychelles.

Clive left him in the care of Kolkata Zoo 130 years ago, where he lived in tranquillity for the last of his 255 years.

But how would I feel about living in constant pain, or lacking my faculties, or without any little dignity I may currently have?

Would I be prepared to be a burden on whoever was prepared to care for me? These are all reasonable questions, that anyone approaching decrepitude must ask.

I was curious enough myself to seek a little information about Dignitas, the Swiss assisted-dying establishment for suicide tourism.

Dignitas was founded in 1998 by a Swiss lawyer and in March 2008, he stated that they had assisted 840 people to die, 60% of them Germans.

Most people coming to Dignitas do not, in fact, plan to die but want to consider options in case their illness becomes intolerable.

In fact 70% never return to Dignitas. 21% of people receiving assisted death in Dignitas do not have a terminal or progressive illness, but rather "weariness of life".

They charge 4,000 Euros for preparation and suicide assistance, but for an additional fee will take over family duties and funerals.

In general, Dignitas offers a pentobarbital overdose that depresses the central nervous system, causing you to become drowsy and fall asleep within ten minutes. Anaesthesia progresses to coma and death is caused by respiratory arrest which occurs within about 30 minutes.

Dignitas are apparently very professional about having patients take private consultations with independent doctors, and legally admissible proof is created in a signed affidavit, with a time gap between two consultations.

Once again, before you are given your lethal overdose, you are asked several times if you wish to proceed, or consider the matter further.

Only after these precautions are taken, and the patient insists on going ahead is the overdose ingested, in a glass of water or orange juice.

Let's hope we never have to see the inside of Dignitas, and can end our lives as pleasantly as Adwaita.

Note: In the UK, on average there is one death from suicide every 85 minutes. Suicide is three times more common amongst men than women. For people aged 15-24, suicide is the second biggest cause of death after road accidents.

J.M.W. Turner *Self-Portrait* circa 1799
One of his minor works sold for almost £30 million at Sotheby's in London, July 2010

WHAT WOULD TURNER DO?

J.M.W. Turner bequeathed 300 of his masterpieces to the nation, alongside 30,000 of his watercolours, drawings and sketches.

Clearly, only a small proportion of his work can be installed in its home at the Tate, and so most of it is never seen by the public, but safely stored away in silent darkness.

I wonder how Turner would feel now, in an age of mass travel and mass communication to have his work squirrelled away, and inaccessible to anyone but scholars.

I think if we were able to ask Turner if he would prefer to have, say, 25,000 of the watercolours and drawings spread around the world's great museums, with large archive centres in Paris, New York, Washington, Berlin, Rome, and the major museums in China, India, Brazil, Australia, South Africa, Russia – don't you think he would prefer it?

Perhaps even 50 or so of his great paintings shared out for each museum to display in their own collection?

I don't know any artist who wouldn't prefer to have his work visible, and available around the globe; a dozen archives in the world's leading museums for students, critics, writers, anyone, able to study his work, rather than in one largely invisible one.

I'd go further.

How would Turner feel if we parted with some of those 30,000 works to be apportioned amongst the world's great institutions, enabling us to build a war chest to strengthen the nation's core collection of art of the last 100 years?

Turner was well-known for supporting younger artists, hence his choice as the bearer of the Turner Prize gong.

He left a financial legacy which he hoped would be used to support less fortunate artists, planning and designing an almshouse for them in Twickenham.

And before the great and the good of the art world throw up their hands in horror at the mere suggestion of dispersing his legacy – the Charity Commission decreed in 1995 that the Turner Bequest was free of Turner's conditions, and there was no obligation to keep them together.

That being the case why not examine the advantage of sharing some of his great achievement – therefore helping fulfil Turner's true intention of having his works always available to be seen (admittedly not in the Turner Museum he was promised at the time – a promise the government reneged on 22 years after his death), but nonetheless widely visible, rather than hidden from view; the Turners you own, but can't see.

I think he would also share my view that the job of a museum of modern art is to ensure that in decades, even centuries to come, the key works that represent important developments in art are available to be examined by future visitors.

This is hard to pull off with a measly acquisitions budget, and it would have always been wrong for the state to buy very new art cheaply before the artist has proven his worth.

That means you have to build the national collection around art that is by definition validated – and more expensive.

But our own little Occam's Razor leaves us with an inadequate national collection of our own great artists – not enough prime Hockney, Freud, Bacon, Auerbach, not a good collection of British Kitchen Sink painters, or British Pop Art pioneers, like Hamilton, and a weak group of works by the YBA generation.

It is a duty of care for museum managers to ensure that in their term of office they are adequately providing future generations of Britons with the ability to see our own outstanding artists well-represented.

With the kind of money raised by spreading our Turners around, we could retain the premier collection of Turner that his bequest provided – and yet allow Britain to acquire enough masterpieces of 20th-century art to rival MoMA. Britain is woefully lacking in a broad spread of top quality works by Manet, Picasso, Cézanne, Malevich, Brancusi and many, many other key artists – all financially out of reach and all vital for a national collection as important as ours.

Turners could be traded with other museums for their own masterpieces by artists they themselves hold in some depth; they could manage to give up one or two in order to achieve the Holy Grail of a powerful Turner collection of their own that they would be able to display.

Even a staunch admirer of Turner, the redoubtable art critic Brian Sewell, wrote at the time the Tate was mounting its campaign to save *The Blue Rigi* painting from being sold abroad – "This is just bloody silly. We have 20,000 Turners in this country and we do not need to spend £5 million to keep *The Blue Rigi* or indeed any of the Rigis."

I think that J.M.W. would be keen to see his bequest gathering a worldwide audience instead of gathering dust; kept together not in a storage facility, but across our world's greatest museums.

As an artist who travelled widely himself to paint, he would probably hope that in this day of global fluidity, his work could be accessible to as many people as possible, everywhere.

He would also have been proud that he alone had made it possible for his homeland to have the spectacularly good national collection of the world's modern masterpieces it deserves.

A further twist in the Turner tale is that after all the public donations were raised for keeping *The Blue Rigi* in Britain, we have ended up keeping it in storage.

Note: I received a letter from J.M.W.'s great-great-niece, Rosalind Mallord Turner, Vice President of The Turner Society, who although at odds with my view that Turner would have wanted his work dispersed across the globe, nevertheless shared a profound concern that so little of Turner's Bequest is on display, and that the Clore Gallery is not meeting its benefactor's intention to provide a permanent home for Turner's masterpieces, and has simply been annexed into an annexe for Tate Britain.

Detail of *St Paul the Hermit*, Jusepe Ribera, 1640

SOCIALIZING FOR PARTY DUDS.

Standing around at a cocktail party, taxi waiting to take me on to the next cocktail party, and then two more cocktail parties after that.

I know some people enjoy this lifestyle, but I can't pull it off and I'm aware that it's my loss being such a dud, and a little late for me to enroll in Socializing For Beginners classes.

I am lost in admiration for friends who are at ease walking into a crowded soirée, and chatting happily as they work the room.

How are you on social etiquette? When do you do handshakes, or kisses, or two kisses? When do you hug? What do you do if you've only met someone once? Is there any clear international guideline e.g. two kisses for someone you've met a few times before or know well, a handshake for someone you meet for the first time, cordial handshake and shoulder pat when they leave?

I fumble around with a hand extended as someone leans in for a hug. I kiss a woman on the cheek as a greeting, then realize belatedly she is offering up her other cheek as well. I never know whether to stand if I am seated at a restaurant and an acquaintance comes by to exchange pleasantries.

I am not fond of receiving a double hand clasp accompanied by a direct penetrating stare, and an immediate repetition of my first name for someone's memory bank, who has studied Dale Carnegie's *How to Win Friends* a little too eagerly.

Psychology Today's Gretchen Rubin once once published a useful guide to social awkwardness and the fear of being the dull person at a party. It made the point that the problem is clearly widespread and can be easily observed:

1) Repeated, perfunctory responses

Your listener who repeats "Oh really? Wow", "Oh really? Interesting", isn't particularly engaged.

2) Simple questions

People who are bored ask simple questions "When did you move?", "Where did you go?" People who are interested ask more complicated questions that show curiosity, not mere politeness.

3) Interruption

Although it sounds rude, interruption is not necessarily a bad sign, often meaning that a person is bursting to say something, thereby showing interest.

4) Request for clarification

A person who is sincerely interested in what you are saying will ask you to elaborate or to explain: "What does that expression mean?", "When exactly did that happen?", "Then what did he say?", are the kinds of questions that show that someone is trying to closely follow your conversation.

5) Imbalance of talking time

Many people fondly suppose that because they do most of the talking, people find them fascinating. In general though, people who are interested in a subject have things to say themselves; they want to add their own opinions, information and experiences. If they are not doing that, they're probably keeping quiet in the hope the conversation will end more quickly.

6) Abrupt changes in topic

If you're talking to somebody about, say, the life of Winston Churchill, and all of a sudden the person asks "So how are your kids?", it's a sign that the person isn't very interested, or perhaps is not listening at all.

7) Audience posture

People slouch or lean when bored, attentive people fidget less, and are less squirmy. Remember if you're bored, there's a good chance the other person may be bored too.

But only if you are truly desperate are you allowed to bring up any of the topics below:

1) A dream
2) Recent changes in your child's nap schedule
3) The route you took to get here
4) An excellent meal you once had at a restaurant
5) Details about your exercise regime
6) An account of your last golf game
7) The plot of a movie, in particular, the funny parts.

One of the unspoken realities of many people's lives is loneliness. Do you believe that humans need close relationships with others to be content and happy, or do you feel many people can feel lonely even surrounded by crowds of friends?

Solitude may suit some people, but obviously only if they are perfectly happy with their own company.

I don't much care for mine, so was intrigued to discover the number of towns and villages around the world with five or fewer residents:

Darlings Beach, Canada
Whitney, Maine, USA
Funkley, Minnesota, USA
Hoot Owl, Oklahoma, USA
Navalsaz, Spain

There are quite a number of extremely small townships like these all over the world. Do you think the residents like solitude, or are just very picky about their neighbours? Do they hang out together each evening, or get together only at Christmas?

If this book ever reaches Funkley, will one of you there please let me know. In the spirit of inclusiveness, perhaps someone would be thoughtful enough to introduce the sole resident of Polana, a village in Northern Poland, to the only inhabitant of Dix's Grant in New Hampshire, USA, also with a population of one. They could, perhaps, exchange the odd postcard.

Having friends round for supper can be perfectly enjoyable. Only occasionally do I find that hospitality is about making your guests feel at home, even if you wish they were.

And remember – a friend is someone who will help you move house. A real friend is someone who will help you move a body.

My mum was fond of reminding me 'Life may not be the party we hoped for, but while we're here, we should dance'.

I always found this analogy strangely callous, as she knew full well I simply cannot dance.

Note: Dale Carnegie's *How to Win Friends and Influence People* was first published in 1936 and still ranks high on Amazon's Bestseller lists. Carnegie wrote "The ideas I stand for are not mine. I borrowed them from Socrates. I swiped them from Chesterfield. I stole them from Jesus. And I put them in a book. If you don't like their rules whose would you use?"

An engraving of an early natural history museum, Naples, 1599

ARE MUSEUMS FOOLING THE PUBLIC, OR THEMSELVES?

Lovely to stroll around our museums, for free.

Not so nice to find that once you have been sucked in with no admission charge, that the exhibition you want to see costs a tenner or more to enter.

It's irritating for the visitor, and perplexing.

Are museums being elitist, and feel that only people who are prepared to pay the £10, £12, £14 admission are worthy of seeing shows by their selected artists?

No, no, museum directors would argue – we have to charge for admission to our exhibitions in order to finance the running costs of the museum, the transportation and insurance of the exhibited works, the cost of installing the show etc.

But even London's leading museums, admirable in so many ways, only earn about 7% of their annual costs from ticket sales – the rest being provided from the public purse, and a little bit from sponsorship. One of the museums I love visiting for example, the Tate, raises just £6.9 million from admission charges set against its running costs of £98.5 million.

Why bother fleecing the public for such a piddling contribution, when the taxpayer is already funding the great bulk of your costs in any event – it's simply double taxation on paying visitors.

I may not know much about finance, with a 'Fail' in GCSE maths, but I do know that attendance at our own gallery could drop by 50% if we charged admission.

Perhaps this is because our audience is often the young, and they are not always the affluent.

Being free-entry for all exhibitions has allowed us to offer five of the six most visited shows in London over the last two years, in the *Art Newspaper's* survey of museum attendance.

I may be a full-blown egocentric, and deeply self-serving, but I do not believe that this is because people flock to share my taste in art.

Neither do I believe that more people are interested in seeing our shows of new art from India, or the Middle East, or Germany, or even the UK, than they are seeing a Rothko retrospective at the Tate Modern. Or Picasso at the National Gallery. Or David Hockney Portraits at the National Portrait Gallery.

And yet we attract many visitors because people don't wish to fork out the whacking entry charges to these important shows.

It is a generally held view that had these spectacular exhibitions been free, attendance would have probably quadrupled.

If for example, the Rothko retrospective had open admission, don't you agree that sales of catalogues, posters, key rings, notepads, teacups, badges, calendars, tea towels, general collectables and knick-knacks, would have doubled, tripled, or indeed also quadrupled, and there is a good chance that the income produced could have been as great as that raised by charging for entry?

This may be just hypothesis, but it's an estimate that is shared by a number of managers of the vast retail outlets at our leading museums.

They feel, as I do, that the Hayward Gallery for example, would have received far more visitors than the 63,000 who visited their Warhol show in 2009, with a £10 entrance charge, compared to the 360,000 who visited *Unveiled*, our show of new art from the Middle East.

The numbers would have been reversed if we had charged £10 entrance, and the Hayward show had been free – and they would probably have made a great deal more profit from having blockbuster retail sales of Warholania than they accrued from ticket sales.

It may also be true that if museums weren't featherbedded by state funding, and focused on maximising their public appeal, they would discover income from sponsors would be easier to attract.

It's easy to see why — sponsors like to back popular well-attended exhibitions; the promotional budgets they hand over to museums then offer greater, more tangible value.

Of course one of the drawbacks of heavily attended exhibitions is that visitors feel short-changed by the crowds milling around the key works; the experience of viewing a big-name show is often unpleasant, claustrophobic, and destroys any hope of experiencing the works in any thoughtful way.

Museums would find that if they stay open in the evenings until 10pm many nights, a lot of overcrowding evaporates and people are able to enjoy the works at times that suit them; we use after-hours to give our 500,000 gallery members, Facebook and Twitter followers, their own late nights.

We also open in the evenings for reader promotions with newspapers and magazines, to spread the load of visitors as widely as possible, so weekends aren't too over-stuffed.

The worst of all museum sins, in my view, is to charge schools for their pupils to see their shows.

From our own experiences, state schools have no budget to pay for their students' entry. Only private schools can manage it, often by asking parents to cover costs of school trips.

The Tate's standard rate for pupils in primary and secondary education is £5 per head for school groups of 10 pupils or more, and the National Portrait Gallery charges £9 per head, or more depending on the exhibition, for pupils in groups of 20.

I'm truly not trying to pick a fight with the Art Gods. I simply think something got screwed up with a policy of keeping museums free — and then frustrating visitors by charging them for entry to the shows they most wish to see.

I like to think that museum directors are not elitist, would like to attract the widest possible audience, and are up to the challenge of managing their museum's affairs – so that the widest number of us can benefit.

Of course I could be wrong, and they are just snooty types, who don't want a lot of riff-raff around. Or worse, they could be so removed from reality that they can't quite follow that £20 is a bit much even for a professional couple to part with every time they want to take in a show.

Note: The Rothko Chapel is a non-denominational chapel in Houston, Texas founded by legendary collectors John and Dominique de Menil. The interior serves not only as a chapel, but also as a major work of modern art. On its walls are fourteen black but colour-hued paintings by Mark Rothko. The shape of the building, an octagon inscribed in a Greek cross, and the design of the chapel was largely inspired by the artist.

The Sumo wrestler Abumatsu Rokunosuke in a woodblock print by Utagawa Kunisada 1786–1864

WOULD YOU RATHER KEEP FIT, OR KEEP ALIVE?

Jim Fixx was the author of a 1977 best seller *The Complete Book of Running*, which is credited with starting the revolution that made running and jogging a regular aspect of many people's daily routine.

In July 1987, Fixx died at the age of 52 from a heart attack after his daily run. His death may have been an unfortunate coincidence, though why take the chance of exerting yourself in any avoidable way?

Many people cycle or swim to keep trim. But if swimming is so good for the figure, how do you explain whales?

I used to cycle for mile after mile as an 11-year-old boy, setting off early in the morning, along the main arterial roads towards Wales or the South Coast, without a care in the world about over-tired truckers, or zonked out drivers swatting me under their wheels.

Parents in those days didn't have views about the health and safety of their offspring, and neither did the offspring.

I gave up my bike when I had my head turned by a young Scottish lass, with a full-on Glasgow accent, who was far more appealing than saddle sores.

Haven't picked up a bicycle since, so completely pain-free buttocks you will be pleased to know.

Although your health is more important than money or success, always remember that good health is merely the slowest possible rate at which you can die. Many people give up their health to gain their wealth, and then give up their wealth to regain their health.

Have you ever had a hankering to try Extreme sports, like paragliding or bungee jumping?

Neither have I. But I like the sound of Extreme Ironing where you take an ironing board to a remote location and iron items of clothing.

Competitors have travelled to mountainsides with their ironing boards, ironed in a canoe, while skiing or snowboarding, on top of large bronze statues, underwater, on busy roads, while parachuting, and while bungee jumping. Working solo or in groups, ironing devotees can be found all over the world.

The sport was pioneered in Leicester in the UK, by Phil Stow, who operates his iron using his epithet 'Steam'.

It has now entered the mainstream, and according to the official website, "extreme ironing is the latest danger sport that combines the thrills of a hazardous outdoor activity with the satisfaction of a well-pressed shirt."

I have to admit to having adolescent fantasies of competing in many different sports, rather brilliantly. Well, not the Bull Run in Pamplona, Spain, where thrill-seekers run alongside a pack of bulls through the cobbled streets of the city to the bullring. Pamplona's finest young men are routinely tossed and gored by the very pointy horns of the 1,000lbs fighting bulls.

Of course, if you really want to demonstrate your manly fitness, you can enter the Wife Carrying tournaments in Finland.

You are obliged to carry your wife, or somebody else's, through an obstacle course, in the fastest time.

The prize takes into account the wife's weight, and she will be carried around the 253.5 metre track, and across a metre deep water trench.

The sport now has an enthusiastic following in the United States, Hong Kong and India, though the world champions for the last three years have been Finns Taisto Miettinen and Kristiina Haapanen. However, Estonian couples were winners in the previous ten world championships.

I asked my wife if she would be prepared to be carried (not by me, naturally) and she is thinking about it, as there is a special prize for the best costume.

I probably still bear the humiliation of never having been picked for any school cricket or football game, unless the need to make up a full squad was a desperate one.

I enjoy many sports enthusiastically, but horizontally, lying in front of the TV – particularly Sumo Wrestling.

When I was morbidly obese for a couple of years, I was transfixed by the life of a Sumo wrestler.

Whereas an average daily intake of about 3,000 calories is the norm for an adult male, mine was probably 6,000 delightful calories a day during my fat years.

Sumos consume 20,000 calories a day, split between two very large meals of 10,000 each.

By sleeping immediately after a meal, a wrestler's body is able to process the food slowly for storage, as fat.

They will also consume at least six pints of beer per meal, with each traditional dish of Chankonabe, a particularly hearty stew.

Despite the diet, and being hurled around in the endless practise bouts during training, and the number of competitive tournaments required to achieve high rankings in the sport, life expectancy for Sumo wrestlers is between 60-65, merely 10 years shorter than the average Japanese male.

Fatties in Britain are regularly told how obesity puts their lives at risk, and are warned about the perilous health risks.

Perhaps it's the perpetual afternoon naps that give the Sumos a surprisingly more lengthy life than I assumed.

My favourite politician Winston Churchill was once asked "Mr. Churchill, sir, to what do you attribute your success in life?" Without time for pause or hesitation, he replied "Conservation of energy. Never stand up when you can sit down, and never sit down when you can lie down." He then got into a chauffeured limousine.

The Arnolfini Portrait, Jan Van Eyck, 1434

LOVE MAY BE BLIND, BUT MARRIAGE IS AN EYE-OPENER.

My favourite philosopher, Cher, said that the trouble with some women is that they get all excited about nothing, and then marry him.

In general marriage is a flawed ideology, with a miserable track record, and only gives comfort to the insecure and needy, like me.

It is often the case that men marry women with the hope they will never change, and women marry men with the hope that they will.

I received a delightful mixed message once: I'm so miserable without you, it's as though you're still here.

The children are also quick to remind me that the cause of a previous divorce was based on religious grounds – I thought I was God and she didn't. But she was just jealous that the voices only spoke to me.

I have been married three times, so far. We all know the thing about second marriages being a triumph of hope over experience, but then once one makes a habit of getting married, it seems a bit rude to go out with anyone and not marry them.

So it's just as well I never dated Katherine Knight, who stabbed her husband 37 times with a butcher's knife before skinning him, decapitating him and cooking him for the children's supper. She prepared the cooked body parts with baked potatoes, pumpkin, cabbage, yellow squash and gravy. Police found the macabre meal before the children arrived home. She was the first Australian woman to be sentenced to life imprisonment without parole.

Equally, I could have been married to Stacey Castor, who fed antifreeze to her husband over 4 days, and then staged the scene to make it appear a suicide. Detectives investigating suspected foul play, exhumed the body of Stacey's first husband, who had supposedly died of a heart attack, and found the same ethylene glycol from antifreeze in his remains. Stacey had a back-up plan however. She arranged the evidence to point the finger at her daughter Ashley, accusing her of killing both her father and stepfather, even though Ashley would have been eleven when husband No.1 died. Stacey is serving 25 years to life.

It seems that I have been more fortunate than I deserve in my chronicle of spouses.

And obviously many past girlfriends have dumped me before I got a chance to propose. I remember one young lady expressed her views particularly succinctly: "You have the IQ of lint, and the thought that terrifies me most is that someone may hate me the way I loathe you. What you lack in intelligence, you more than make up for in stupidity. Someday you will find yourself, and you will wish you hadn't. I worship the ground that awaits you, you snake".

I was so impressed by her withering review, that I asked for another chance, which she wisely rejected.

Many, many other humiliations left me crestfallen, but thankfully have been forgotten. This particular one seems to haunt me still.

I was 17, arrived home a little drunk, and a little desperate, and our au pair's bedroom was down the hall.

She was a very blonde Scandinavian, but truly, madly obese, and her B.O. would startle a horse.

As I possibly mentioned, I was a teeny bit desperate, knocked on her door, and she was delightfully welcoming, as I made a fumbling attempt at a clinch.

The smell was overpowering even in my fevered state, and her body was perhaps a little too spectacularly fulsome, but I suggested that a bath together might be romantic. She looked puzzled but readily agreed.

Sorry to reveal that I passed out in the bath, and the incident was never to be discussed again.

But we both knew what an utter twerp I was. Helga, if you see this, I'm so sorry.

But what is wrong with trying anything and everything that is available to secure an acceptable mate?

If the ends don't justify the means, what does?

My pal Steve used to arrange 4 meetings a night every hour between 7 and 10, so that he didn't have time to be haunted by self-doubt if things went poorly. Even if he met someone nice, he didn't appear too desperate, as he had to move on to the next rendezvous on the schedule.

He was resilient, and could handle disappointment well (girls pretending to be very ill 2 minutes after meeting him, girls pretending to receive an emergency call on their mobile before he's finished his first chat-up line).

His view was, if you can handle the humiliation, you will meet some interesting people and hopefully someone to settle down happily with, and have many babies, just as he has.

One of my friends was so deranged by his wife's nagging, even though it was conducted in a caring and tactful manner, that he told me about his discovery of the "brank".

This was perfected in sixteenth century Scotland, where it was also known as the "scold's bridle", an iron muzzle in a framework that enclosed the head, and clamped the tongue. If a woman was considered shrewish or too gossipy, the brank would be fitted, making it impossible to speak.

It proved so effective, it quickly gained popularity in England.

Today, it would probably be considered inappropriate by Health & Safety officials, so he could simply ask his wife to wear it only at home.

Of course, one of my greatest fears is to meet ex-girlfriends from my teenage years, who are tottering little old ladies, like me.

And with my track record of divorces, the only advice I can usefully offer a friend whose marriage is in difficulty is to remind him that wives make excellent housekeepers: They always manage to keep the house. Boom boom!

Jean Sibelius in the 1945 photograph by Karsh

TAKE A LESSON FROM THE WEATHER.
IT PAYS NO ATTENTION TO CRITICISM.

The revered Finnish composer Sibelius once consoled a young musician after a poorly-received concert. "Remember, my boy", he said patting him on the shoulder, "there is no city in the world where they have erected a monument of a critic."

I have an idiosyncratic relationship with reviews. If they're approving, I fear that the exhibition must be pedestrian. If they're disobliging, I feel for the critic, who is clearly unenlightened about contemporary art, insecure about a lack of visual perceptiveness, a crabby soul, for whom it would be a kindness to cut short a morose, sour life. A perfectly balanced perspective, as you can see. I bore myself to a stupor in a self-pitying whinge about good shows that get caned, or worse, overlooked (like our final show at Boundary Road of the eviscerating work by the Russian photographer Boris Mikhailov, that got absolutely no reviews and about four visitors). So the truth is, even a thorough shredding of an exhibition means that at least the critics have been kind enough to cover it, if only to cover it in bile.

I richly deserve the thorough kicking I still regularly receive for an exhibition we produced in 1999, *Neurotic Realism*. It was a critical failure of my own making, caused by giving it a title that whiffed of an over-arching effort to create a new art movement, rather than a feeble attempt to find a catchy show title. But in some defence, the exhibition did introduce the work of Ron Mueck, Noble & Webster, Cecily Brown, Dexter Dalwood, Martin Maloney, Michael Raedecker, all of whom went on to international acclaim. If I hadn't come up with such a clunker of a name, they would probably have got more favourable attention at the time, rather than having my own poor judgement get in the way.

People are fond of saying that most art critics were failures as artists.

But of course there is no such thing as a failed artist. Either their work is not very good, or nobody very good has looked at it. The task is daunting and precarious, with very few achieving commercial success; often however, the effort yields its own reward.

In the UK we have so many newspapers carrying lengthy art reviews that most shows find themselves getting a mixed bag of responses, and no one critic matters that much, whatever their credentials. My favourite, Brian Sewell, has never written a favourable word about any show I've done in 20 years, but dismisses them with such grandeur and refinement, it's almost flattering to be duffed up by him. The days when critics could create an art movement by declaring the birth of 'Abstract Expressionism', Clement Greenberg-style, are firmly over.

People tell me that a Roberta Smith review in *The New York Times* carries some weight, but that's because it's the only paper in town. Ms Smith has been looking at art as hard and as long as anyone, so she mostly knows what she is seeing (not too patronising I hope, Roberta).

But, in reality Americans believe *The New York Times* is created each day by God and its sonorous tone accords it absolute authority. So with rich New Yorkers being notoriously insecure about their art collecting, a respectful review offers great reassurance. Or so I thought. It seems that in recent years the main driving force for much collecting has been the giddy rush to board the gravy train as prices for contemporary art rocket ever higher. The critics don't get a look-in any more.

But nobody does criticism like John Simon, the illustrious New York film and theatre commentator. Here's his charming review of Elizabeth Taylor as Katherina in *The Taming Of The Shrew*: 'Just how garish her commonplace accent, squeakily shrill voice, and the childish petulance with which she delivers her lines, my pen is neither scratchy nor leaky enough to convey.' I am obviously delighted he doesn't cover art for a British newspaper. Sometimes a horrific review can turn out to be quite helpful. The *Sensation* exhibition was so universally panned, it aroused curiosity and ended up doing well for the Royal Academy's box office receipts.

And critic Eugene Field made an instant celebrity of one hapless actor with this notice: 'Last night Mr Creston Clarke played King Lear at the Tabor Grand. All through the five acts of that Shakespearean tragedy he played the King as though under momentary apprehension that someone else was about to play the Ace'.

Savage reviews are satisfying for the pundit, who gets to show off his rapier wit, and entertaining for the reader. Only the subject of the review is temporarily chastened, and rarely is a critic found garrotted or battered to death by one of his enraged victims. But remember, before you criticize someone you should walk a mile in their shoes. That way when you criticize them, you are a mile away, and you have their shoes.

All you need to know about most art experts, art curators and art critics is that for 47 days in 1961, Matisse's *Le Bateau* was hanging upside down in the Museum of Modern Art, New York. Apparently none of the 34 of the Museum's curatorial staff, nor 280 art critics, noticed. The mistake was spotted by a member of the public, Genevieve Hubert, a stockbroker.

I was once asked if I could recall the most biting criticism someone has made of me, something that I had to accept was painfully accurate. I'm sure there were worse, but I remembered one: 'He's alright in his own way, as long as he always gets it.'

Someone else was keen to point out that I have 'shoddy taste in art and simply promote artists who are second-rate, buying them on the cheap, and turning them into valuable commodities to cash in on.' 'Furthermore,' they argued, 'your so-called discoveries, the Damien Hirsts, the Jenny Savilles, etc. would have found success just as well without you buying up their art. Critics also think that your influence on younger artists is damaging, and encourages the view that it is more important to produce visually striking work, and achieve overnight success, than to carefully hone their technical skills to a professional standard.' I couldn't think of an adequate response other than to thank him for sharing.

Thomas Edison – "Too stupid to learn anything."

GOOD IS THE ENEMY OF GREAT?

This well-worn motivation-speak mantra is intended to spur people ever upwards.

It is foolhardy nonsense.

Greatness is the preserve of the very few, and being good at something is an achievement that shouldn't be sniffed at. Many talented people become unglued in an obsessive/compulsive pursuit of perfection. The entire canon of self-improvement literature is of course reliant on ambushing our insecurities and inadequacies and propelling us on a fast-track to success and fulfilment. However ironic your reading of the advice on offer, it is touching in its optimism:

You must remain focused on your journey to greatness.

Don't wish it were easier; wish you were better.

Don't wish for fewer problems, wish for more skills.

Do not wait for your ship to come in – swim out to it.

Success is not to be pursued; it is to be attracted by the person you have become.

Many of these invaluable guidelines, including *Good is the Enemy of Great* which was borrowed from Voltaire, are offered by self-help guru Jim Rohn, who helped himself to a splendid fortune by dispensing acres of motivational wisdom to hopeful Americans.

Fortunately one of his audience took a slightly askance view from Jim's, and wrote his own bestseller *How to be a Complete & Utter Failure in Life, Work and Everything: 44½ Steps to Lasting Underachievement*, which I imagine was more spiritually uplifting in every way.

Failure is no obstacle to success.

Henry Ford had his first five businesses fail, leaving him broke each time, before he founded the Ford Motor Company.

Soichiro Honda was turned down for a job as an engineer at Toyota, and after a long period of unemployment he started making scooters in his home, and his friends persuaded him to start a business selling them.

Bill Gates dropped out of Harvard and his first business 'Traf-O-Data', failed. He eventually started again with a new idea, Microsoft.

Akio Morita's first venture for his fledgling business was a rice cooker, that burnt rice rather than cooked it, and sold less than 100 units. His tiny company, Sony, struggled but survived.

Colonel Sanders of Kentucky Fried Chicken had his famous secret chicken recipe rejected over 1000 times before a restaurant accepted.

Walt Disney was fired by a newspaper editor because "he lacked imagination and had no good ideas". He started a number of businesses that all ended in failure and bankruptcy, before he invented Mickey Mouse.

The good news for parents of children who don't seem overly bright is that Albert Einstein did not speak until he was four, and did not read until he was seven. He was expelled from school, and was refused acceptance to Zurich Polytechnic.

Thomas Edison was told by teachers he was "too stupid to learn anything". He was fired from his first two jobs for not being productive enough. Edison made over 1000 attempts at inventing the light bulb, before one of his ideas worked.

Stephen King's first book *Carrie* received 30 rejections, causing King to give up and throw it in the rubbish bin. His wife rescued it and encouraged him to keep submitting it. He is now one of the bestselling authors of all time.

In 1954 Elvis Presley was fired from the Grand Ole Opry after just one performance, the manager telling him "You ain't goin' nowhere, son. You ought to go back to drivin' a truck". He had his first number one hit 2 years later.

Most people only got to the top after scraping along at the bottom.

Failure is very disagreeable, but the bitter taste of it is often the finest spur to claw your way to success.

In 1889, the editor of the *San Francisco Examiner*, having published one article by Rudyard Kipling, declined to accept any more of the author's work. "I'm sorry, Mr. Kipling" he explained, "but you just don't know how to use the English language. This isn't a kindergarten for amateur writers."

Eight years later, Kipling, who had already written *The Man Who Would Be King*, in 1888, was awarded the Nobel Prize for Literature.

One day perhaps you will be able to emulate George Bernard Shaw, who early in his career, had his request to stage a play repeatedly declined by a certain producer.

Years later, Shaw, by then a highly successful playwright, was amused to receive a telegram from the producer, offering to stage the same, previously rejected work.

Shaw promptly cabled his reply: "Better never than late."

Let me admit now that I wouldn't make much of being a publisher. I would certainly have returned James Joyce's work as impenetrable, but greatly admired his response to questions about the effort his writing required to be properly grasped. "The only demand I make of my reader" he replied, "is that he devote his whole life to reading my work."

The list of literary giants, or simply best-selling authors whose works were rejected by dozens of publishers before they found the one that didn't, is a lengthy one.

So even if your novel is a work of genius, being passed over by publisher after publisher is par for the course. And if your work is less than good, judgement in the publishing world is clearly so unpredictable, you may yet find a home for your novel, and achieve an Amazonian success.

Even I, after all, managed to sell you a copy of this book.

Chartres Cathedral, 1830, Oil on canvas, Camille Corot

WAS ROTHKO CLOSER TO GOD THAN US?

For some people Rothko's work resonates with spirituality. They say it evokes 'infinity'.

My understanding of infinity goes something like this: every 100 years a sparrow flies to the top of a large mountain, and cleans its beak by scraping it on the highest rock. By the time the mountain has been scraped away to a small pile of dust, that would be the equivalent of the first second of infinity.

I thought of that the last time I stood in front of a Rothko and neither felt an overwhelming sense of infinity, nor had a mystical experience of any kind. Maybe I've just seen too many Rothkos and they don't pulsate with ethereal splendour for me anymore. Or perhaps I never quite got the wonder of Rothko.

Of course, people seeking spiritual inspiration can find it more traditionally, in the world's great cathedrals.

Chartres is my favourite, and like its competitors in any listings of World's Great Places Of Worship, it does the job of inspiring shock and awe at the omnipotence of religion.

They are all equally powerful expressions of the humbleness of the individual in the presence of the Almighty, and one can see why religious belief has held such sway for so long, and inspired much hatred and war, as well as succour.

I'd be perfectly happy to convert to Catholicism if I could hold my next marriage ceremony at Chartres, but I gather they don't go in for divorcees, particularly serial ones.

Maybe I could try the Sedlec Ossuary in the Czech Republic. It is renowned for the artistically arranged bones from the skeletons of over

40,000 people, to form decorations, furnishings and chandeliers for the chapel.

Apparently in 1870 František Rint, a woodcarver, was employed by the family who owned the chapel to put the heaps of bones and skeletons that had been collected since the Black Death in the 14th century, and over many subsequent wars, into some order. The macabre result now attracts 200,000 visitors yearly.

Do you believe Christianity, Catholicism in particular, will grow or decline in the next 50 years?

To me, the enduring power of the Church appears inexhaustible.

I heard that there are many churches in Antarctica, including Russian orthodox, Bulgarian orthodox, a non-denominational Christian chapel, several Catholic chapels, including one made entirely of ice at Belgrano base.

They do say Belief keeps you warm in the most bitter of conditions.

There are also churches built into a tree (a 1,000 year-old oak with a 15metre base houses a chapel in Allouville, France), into cliff-sides, bridges, salt mines, caves, and even underground in South Australia, where you will find a Serbian Orthodox church.

Many people find meditation plays an important part in their lives. I did check into the amount of time necessary to achieve inner peace, and it makes the prospect a little daunting for me.

You are hopefully a more receptive candidate, so you should choose a Mantra, and I can offer you a sample to select from: Om, or Chivo Ham, or Thiru Neela Kantam, or Om Mani Padme Hum, all of which represent the Supreme Being; these sacred syllables are said to satisfy every need and lead to liberation.

You must repeat your Mantra every day in multiples of 108 (Mantra beads are helpful in keeping track of the number of repetitions you have done). Do this each day and the Mantra will repeat in your mind without any conscious instigation on your part, outside of your specified meditation time.

You are advised to repeat the Mantra at other times, walking, taking a shower, doing the dishes. Put yourself to sleep at night repeating the Mantra, and wake up with your Mantra.

As your Mantra must connect you with the sacred, select one that resonates with the area of your life or quality you most wish to enhance.

Good luck, go in peace, live long and prosper, and may the force of Vashikaran be with you.

Religious belief brings with it many obstacles, unpredictable and troubling to some. Christmas festivities were a bit of a hurdle for Nazi ideologists to overcome during the Third Reich; they believed that Christian elements had been superimposed on traditional Germanic customs.

Christmas Eve, they argued, had nothing to do with the birth of Jesus Christ, a Jew. In essence, it celebrated the winter solstice, and the rebirth of the sun —the swastika was an ancient symbol of the sun and should be placed at the top of fir trees during the festivities.

Father Christmas was a distortion of the Germanic god Odin, and it was Odin who was seen on seasonal posters, riding a white charger, with a long grey beard, bearing a sackful of gifts.

Christian carols were changed, so that *Silent Night* made no mention of God, Christ or religion.

Mary and Jesus were depicted as a blonde mother and child, obviously.

And of course the Christmas festival in itself was to be referred to as 'Julfest', referring to the yuletide that had been usurped by Christians from the historical Germanic and Norse populations.

You will be glad to know that Christmas and Santa are back and thriving in post-Hitler Germany.

And that Germans really adore Rothko, and have little problem embracing the spirituality of his paintings.

Franz Liszt, 1811–1886

THE BEATLES DIDN'T CREATE BEATLEMANIA.
IT WAS FRANZ LISZT.

Long before Beatlemania, I remember Lisztomania, and the delirium that surrounded Franz Liszt's performance that I attended in Berlin on December 27th, 1841. Liszt's playing raised the mood of the audience to a level of hysterical ecstasy. Admirers of Liszt's would swarm over him, fighting over his handkerchiefs and gloves. Women would try to get locks of his hair, and would wear his portrait on brooches and cameos.

Lisztomania or Liszt Fever, had a much more medical emphasis than Beatlemania, as 'mania', in those times, was held to have far stronger connotations than simply a new popular fashion or craze.

In 1843 a Munich newspaper reported 'Liszt Fever, a contagion that breaks out in every city the pianist visits, and which neither age nor wisdom can protect, seems to appear here more sporadically, and asphyxiating cases such as appeared so often in northern capitals, need not be feared by our residents, with their strong constitutions.'

Beatlemania and Lisztomania are nothing compared to Stendhal Syndrome.

It is officially a medical condition, which I probably suffer from; a psychosomatic illness that causes rapid heartbeat, dizziness, fainting, confusion and even hallucinations when an individual is exposed to art, usually when the art is particularly beautiful, or when large amounts of art are seen together in a single place.

The illness is named after the French author Stendhal's experiences in 1817 when visiting Florence, taking in the masterpieces on display in the Uffizi Museum; it was attributed in this way after an Italian psychiatrist Magherini identified and described more than 100 similar cases amongst visitors to Florence.

Lovers of Wagner are also prone to the condition, and I am certain that were you to speak to the Royal Opera House, they would be able to confirm that Stendhal Syndrome sufferers are regularly in need of treatment in many performances.

I am not a fully committed admirer of Wagner, or indeed very much opera. I can't stand organ music, and can only manage Bach sparingly.

But if you enjoy the sound of the organ, perhaps you could try *Organ²/ASLSP (As SLow aS Possible)* written by John Cage in 1987, the longest lasting musical number yet conceived. Its performance, which started on the St. Burchardi church organ in Halberstadt, Germany in 2001, is scheduled to have a duration of 639 years, ending in 2640.

The score consists of eight pages, the tempo of which has been structured to fit the wanted time duration. John Cage died in August 1992, and the first chord was played in his honour, lasting from February 2003 to July 2005.

Following that was a three-note chord that lasted two years. A new chord took over, (C4-A flat4, for aficionados), but in 2008 weights holding down the pedals were shifted, resulting in a further chord change. The next chord changes will take place on July 5th, 2012, and on October 5th, 2013, if you are in the neighbourhood of Halberstadt, and can drop into St. Burchardi.

Cage, to many the most influential avant-garde composer of the 20th century, is perhaps most revered for his 1952 composition 4'33", the three movements of which are performed without a single note being played.

The content of the composition is meant to be perceived as the sounds of the environment that the listeners hear during its performance, rather than merely as 4 minutes and 33 seconds of silence.

Cage makes the work of his greatest influence, Schoenberg, sound like bubblegum pop in comparison.

For me, however, Stendhal Syndrome only kicks in when I visit one of the world's great art museums.

Even then, I always feel sorry for the paintings, who probably hear more harebrained, batty, nonsensical remarks than anything else on earth.

The links between art and music are manifest, and although artists are influenced by everything, this particular crossover has been clearly highlighted over the years.

For example, Free-form Jazz and Abstract Expressionism both grew alongside each other in post-war America. And the minimal music of Philip Glass, Terry Riley, Steve Reich has obvious parallels with the art of Sol LeWitt, Carl Andre and Donald Judd being made simultaneously in the late 1960s.

I am fortunate to enjoy a great deal of different art as well as a wide variety of music. It would be quicker to tell you the music I like than the music I don't. I love my favourites of 50s and 60s R&R and Girl groups, Bubblegum, Heavy Metal, Blues, Standards, Cajun, Reggae, Rockabilly, R&B, Disco, Soul, Dance, Punk, Doo-Wop, Country, Arab and Indian music, even some Opera and Classical.

In short, I'll take Dr. Dre and Cyndi Lauper alongside Vivaldi and Stockhausen. I don't like: Brass Bands, One-Man Bands, Big Bands, Harps, Mandolins, Peruvian Pipes, Irish Jigs, Church Organs, Bagpipes, Marches, Most Jazz or Folk, Madrigals, Techno or Emo, Gospel or Funk, New Romantics, Europop. I'd prefer John Cage's four and a half minutes of silence.

Wouldn't you like to attend a performance by the First Vienna Vegetable Orchestra?

They are a greatly admired Austrian musical group who use instruments made entirely of fresh vegetables.

The ensemble, founded in 1998, consists of 10 musicians, one cook and one sound technician. The intention was to create a sonorous experience, which can be perceived by all the senses.

Their distinctive repertoire seems to be rooted in sound art, experimental and electronic music, playing unheard of interpretations of

Igor Stravinsky and Kraftwerk, as well as their own compositions.

Instruments are fashioned from inventions they have assembled, including carrot recorders, clappers made from aubergines, trumpets crafted from courgettes, all amplified with specialist microphones.

They are always fabricated just an hour before each performance using the freshest vegetables available, and then all ninety pounds of vegetables are cooked into a soup following the concert, and served to the audience.

If you wish to catch their next appearance, they have an official website, The Vegetable Orchestra, where they will also make available three CDs they have released, *Gemise* 1999, *Automate* 2003 and *Onionoise* 2010.

The musical scope of the orchestra expands as they fuse a number of musical styles – house, free jazz etc, and add new instruments – celery guitars, celeriac bongos, radish and pepper horns, leek violins, pumpkin drums.

What was the first record you ever bought? Personally, I can't remember if it was Sanford Clark's 'The Fool' or 'Reet Petite' by Jackie Wilson, in 1957. 'The Fool' was your basic rockabilly three-chord number with an exceptionally deep echo chamber and an insistent guitar theme running hypnotically throughout. Sanford Clark was a one-hit wonder, who had dreams of becoming Elvis. I loved it, but it was no 'Mystery Train', my favourite Presley record of the time and probably ever.

I spent every second I could tuned into AFN (American Forces Network) on the radio, listening to the music coming out of America from about 1955 – Fats Domino, Bo Diddley – and remember the ecstasy of first hearing 'Maybelline' by Chuck Berry as it headed up the US charts. 'Reet Petite' was written by Berry Gordy, what a guy, who went on to found Motown records. It became a big hit in Britain 29 years later, thanks to being featured in a Levi's commercial, bless them.

Levi's invented the golden oldie backdrop for their TV commercials, courtesy of John Hegarty at his BBH ad agency. John had in fact previously introduced pop music as a background to a jeans commercial, working on another manufacturer for my agency in the early 1970s. He commissioned David Dundas to write something catchy, which turned out to be a little soft-rock number called 'Jeans On', that surprised everyone by going straight to the top of the charts.

Since then commercials featuring pop backgrounds have been a useful way to promote new releases, revive forgotten hits, resurrect forgotten recording stars, and make the adverts memorable.

In more innocent times, most music in commercials used to be those fabulously awful jingles still swirling inside our heads for decades.

Poland's Crooked Forest; the pine trees in this western corner of Poland grow with a 90% bend at the base of their trunks – all directed northward.

COULD YOU DRAW AN ACCURATE MAP OF
EUROPE FROM MEMORY?

Map making is still a precarious enterprise, so don't be downhearted if your drawing of Europe is as cack-handed as mine.

How were we to know that Büsingen am Hochrhein is a German town, though it is entirely contained within Switzerland?

Or that Sealand is a principality, or formally a micronation, that produces its own stamps and money, but is located 10km off the coast of Suffolk, England, with a population that rarely exceeds ten?

Or that Belgium and The Netherlands share a number of municipalities, where homes, offices, factories and shops are resident in both countries simultaneously?

Though I couldn't even draw an embarrassingly idiotic map, I do have a store of useless geographical knowledge to offer.

When I say useless, I mean the fact that the shortest place name on earth is Å, a town bordering Sweden and Norway.

The largest city in the world is Hulunbuir in China, which stretches 102,000 sq miles.

The world's biggest mountain chain on earth is the Mid-Atlantic Ridge, 25,000 miles long, and the only part of the mountain above water is Iceland.

The Andes at only 4,350 miles are the second largest chain, though of course we can see them and clamber over them if we wish, without a snorkel.

I can keep a dinner party rapt for hours with these tantalizing topographical tidbits.

I have never learnt how to swim, in the same way that I learnt nothing much about anything at school, by bunking off swimming classes.

But if you are proud of your swimming abilities, I recommend Lake Nyos in Cameroon, a deep water lake high on the flank of an inactive volcano.

A pocket of magma lies beneath the lake and leaks carbon dioxide into the water, turning it into carbon acid.

In 1986, Lake Nyos suddenly emitted a large cloud of CO2, which suffocated 1,700 people and 3,500 livestock in nearby towns and villages.

It is the first known large-scale asphyxiation caused by a natural event. To prevent reoccurrence, a degassing tube was constructed, which siphons water from the bottom layers of the lake up to the top, allowing the carbon dioxide to leak in safe quantities.

Before I encourage you to show off your backstroke there, I should point out the lake also poses a threat due to its weakening outer natural wall, which could give way and allow the carbon dioxide to flood out.

However, I am sure a powerful swimmer like you will be perfectly fine.

When people return from a vacation to Africa or Australia, they are often astounded at how different the vastness of the sky seems there, how radiant it is with thousands of stars. You don't enjoy this sight in Britain, or indeed anywhere I have been in Europe.

I am not a stargazer, nor do I have a powerful telescope in the garden to admire the various constellations.

But I have enjoyed the Big Sky view people describe, when I travelled over the years, and it was indeed spectacular.

I was surprised to read that the colour of the universe is a slightly beigeish white, which the scientists who identified it in 2001 dubbed 'Cosmic Latte'.

The survey included more than 200,000 galaxies. The overwhelming majority of stars are at least five billion years old; as they would have been brighter in the past, the colour of the universe changes over time, shifting from blue to red as more blue stars change to yellow, and eventually red giants.

As light from distant galaxies reaches the earth, the average colour of the universe increases to a creamy white, also called Cappuccino Cosmico, Big Bang Beige, Cosmic Cream, Skyvory, and Primordial Clam Chowder by a number of fun-loving astronomers.

Did you know that you are able to purchase the right to name a star and give it the official designation of your choice? I know of such a star, named Trixie-Bell Goldmeyer by the proud parents of a newborn daughter. Simply go to StarListings.co.uk.

The testimonials on their site are delightful.

'It was a beautiful present and my friend was over the moon' A.J. Glasgow

Can I help you to create a meaningful legacy, so that you can feel your life has made a worthwhile and memorable contribution to the world?

Bill Gates has had a flower fly, only found in Costa Rica's cloud forests, named after him.

Another fly found in similar habitats was named after Gates' founding Microsoft partner Paul Allen.

The discoverer of these species named them in recognition of "both their great contributions to the science of dipterology".

Inspiring, isn't it?

I can't imagine travelling to the cloud forests of Costa Rica, or pretty much anywhere remote, in search of a rare fly, or anything else for that matter - not even a life-enhancing spiritual experience.

An American friend of mine was planning to travel to Africa, looking to be uplifted by the wild, untamed wilderness, somewhere vast and sparsely populated, to refresh his sense of living life to the full.

I had to break it to him that although the percentage of Africa that is wilderness is 28%, the percentage of North America that is wilderness is 38%.

He could find all the challenge he was seeking far closer to home. And if he got disenchanted with the ascetic tranquility of a less frenetic environment, he was not going to be too far away from a Starbucks.

Modern Rome, 1757, Oil on canvas, Giovanni Paolo Panini

This picture contrived to show the most famous monuments of the city for the Grand Tour, arranged as paintings in a sumptuous gallery.

THE JET SET HAVE FLOWN AWAY.

Do you remember when young girls used to dream of becoming airline stewardesses?

Not so any longer.

There used to be something called the 'Jet Set', in the 50s and 60s, when airline travel was considered chic. Travel these days is no longer glamorous, and flight attendants have to deal with a variety of passengers, not all charming, and constantly having to field fascinating questions.

I cannot imagine the patience required by stewardesses who are asked, regularly:

"Can you open the window please?"

"Do you have a McDonalds on board?"

"Can you direct me to the showers?"

"Can you take my children to the play area?"

Others working with tourists have reported being asked:

"Why on earth did they put Windsor Castle on the flight path to Heathrow?"

"Is Wales closed during Winter?"

"Can you tell me who performs at the circus in Piccadilly?"

"What month is the May Day holiday?"

"Are there supermarkets in Sydney, and can you get milk all year round?"

"Was the Grand Canyon man-made?"

Perhaps young children now have worked out that the Golden Age of Travel, the Grand Tour, the glamour of supersonic flight, are all long gone, and an air hostess is fortunate these days if she is not driven to throw open the airplane hatch and hurl herself out.

Do you get nervous on airplanes?

Fortunately I don't, but I have acquaintances whose fear of flying is so great they only travel by car or train, which is obviously inconvenient for friends and family who want to get to holiday destinations quickly. Even if you didn't suffer from flying phobia, you would be nervy about landing at Indira Gandhi International airport in New Delhi.

"Jackals, nilgais, monitor lizards, peacocks, porcupines, snakes, monkeys, foxes, dogs and birds of prey – the diversity of wildlife at the airport can give a small town zoo a run for its money" reported the *Hindustan Times* in June 2008. Wild animals including deer, pigs and wild boar, stray onto runways at Indian airports regularly, resulting in long delays while they are moved on.

Occasionally an unfortunate aircraft crashes into an equally unfortunate beast, as happened when an Air India flight hit a blue bull while landing at Kanpur airport, and to Kingfisher Airline flights that hit a stray pig on the runway of Ambedkar International airport, and a dog on the runway at HAL Bangalore airport.

However, for most passengers I suppose it is true that if a flight is not delayed, you are not airsick, not nauseated by the food, not placed next to an obese bore, and not hijacked, the journey is perfectly acceptable – provided that you are prepared to be treated like the bovine creatures on Indian airport runways, the moment you set foot in Heathrow.

Before I lost the will to travel, I had immersed myself in the endless joys of Italy, visiting every inch from the Dolomites to the toes; after that I used to time my holidays to immerse myself in the joys of Wimbledon fortnight, and saw so much tennis that nowadays I can only rouse myself to see the great players at work.

I have been to the South of France (vile) and the Croatian coast for our honeymoon (wet, windy, and moving very swiftly into cheesy tat, without the slow build up of, say, St. Tropez, which took 40 years to grow from charming fishing village to WAG hellhole).

Can I mention how lovely London is in August? This is my third year to have the city empty out, and be reinvigorated by trains of tourists walking about in black burkhas clutching black AmEx cards, plus the delightful flood of visitors from the Far East, which continues to provide us with the traditional groups of smiling photographers, snapping away at Buckingham Palace, or pigeons, and fulfilling every cliché.

A friend was in Moscow recently, for the first time since it embraced capitalism. It is a remarkable transformation he told me, with a much happier and exciting atmosphere, but he was amazed at the number of wild dogs roaming the streets.

Muscovites told him they have the biggest population of stray dogs of any world city.

When I researched this a bit, I discovered most strays are apparently not born homeless, but arrive on the streets as rejected or abandoned household pets. There are 35,000 of them roaming Moscow, ranging from the truly wild, feral dogs, mainly nocturnal and who see humans as a threat.

Alongside are 'beggar dogs', the most intelligent, and integrated with people but not affectionate or personally attached, unfazed by high levels of activity around them, even managing to sleep in the midst of busy areas. When they work in packs, they deploy the smaller, cuter members to beg for food, realizing they have most success.

The quantity of food available keeps the number of dogs steady at about the 35,000 mark, the population being self-regulating, with most pups born to strays never reaching adulthood, the ones surviving merely replacing adult dogs that have died.

My favourites of the Moscow dogs are the 500 who live in the Metro, the world's second most heavily used by commuters.

The Metro dogs have learnt to use the system as a means of travelling around the city, and theories abound as to how they are able to correctly determine the routes:

- An ability to judge the length of time spent on the train between stations.
- Registration of the place names announced on their train's loudspeaker.
- The scents of particular stations.
- They are said to prefer the quieter, less trafficked carriages at the very front and back of the train.

Nowadays I am too lazy to travel more than is absolutely vital to keep my marriage intact, and am even too indolent to drive, preferring the delights of a black cab.

I do own a car, a 1995 black Lincoln Town Car, huge, comfy, with just the right amount of mafia don presence. I haven't driven it in years, but thought I might need it one day for an emergency trip to the local A&E if one of my strange children is broken in some way.

Of course when the emergency came (it was raining and I was too lazy to walk the 100 yards to the newsagent) the battery was so shocked at being asked to start the car, it promptly died. So my majestic Lincoln still sits there, unable to do anything much except gather dust and bird droppings.

Note: St. Tropez was the first town on the Mediterranean coast to be liberated during World War II. In the 1950s it became an internationally-known seaside resort renowned principally because of the influx of artists of the French New Wave in cinema and the Yé-yé movement in music. Since Brigitte Bardot made it iconic, it has been the destination of choice for wealthy Europeans and Americans to park their yachts and party.

INCORPORATED UNDER THE LAWS OF THE STATE OF DELAWARE

N.W. Ayer & Son was the first advertising agency in the United States, founded in Philadelphia, Pennsylvania in 1869, and responsible for some of the most enduring slogans in advertising history, including: "When it rains it pours", advertising salt for Morton Salt in 1912. "I'd walk a mile for a Camel", advertising cigarettes for R.J. Reynolds Tobacco, from 1921. "A diamond is forever", advertising diamonds for De Beers, from 1948. "Be all you can be", advertising military service for the United States Army, from 1981.

ADVERTISING IS EASY MONEY FOR SCHOOL DROPOUTS.

At 17 and with two 'O' Levels to show after a couple of attempts, a career path wasn't realistic, nor a chat with the Christ's College Careers Officer, who wouldn't have recognised me in any event as my absenteeism record was unrivalled.

Though I was often advised that hard work pays off in the end, I felt that laziness pays off now.

After a stint at driving the delivery van for the local grocer, I answered a situations vacant ad in the *Evening Standard* for a Voucher Clerk, pay £10 weekly. It was in a tiny advertising agency in Covent Garden, and a voucher clerk had to traipse round all the local newspaper offices in Fleet Street, of which there were hundreds at the time, and pick up back copies of papers in which the agency's clients had an advert appearing. The voucher clerk's role was to get the newspaper, find the ad, stick a sticker on it so the client could then verify its appearance, and the agency could get paid. Vital work, obviously.

One of the advantages of it being a tiny agency is that one day they got desperate when their Creative Department (one young man) was off sick, and they asked me if I could try and make up an ad for one of their clients, Thornber Chicks. This ad was to appear in *Farmer & Stockbreeder* magazine, and hoped to persuade farmers to choose Thornbers, as their chicks would grow to provide many cheap, superior quality eggs and a fine return.

I didn't know how you write an ad, or indeed how to write anything much other than 'I will not be late for Assembly', for which I had been provided much practice. So I looked through copies of *Farmer & Stockbreeder* and *Poultry World*, chose some inspiring-sounding words and phrases, cobbled them together, stuck on a headline – I think I stole it from an old American advertisement – and produced 'Ask the man who owns them' as a testimonial campaign featuring beaming Thornber farmers. The client bought it.

After being rejected for a copy test by J. Walter Thompson, Young & Rubicam, Ogilvy & Mather, and failing at interviews, or to even get an interview at every other agency I could think of, I managed to wriggle my way into an appointment to see Jack Stanley, the creative director of Benton & Bowles.

God knows why he agreed to see me, or what he saw in this gormless youth sat in front of him, but he was American, noted that I seemed mad about all things American and knew a little about American ads, and could start immediately. Literally immediately, because he promptly walked me down a corridor, told me he had hired another young trainee last week, and I was to work with him. Luckily for me the trainee was John Hegarty, and we hit it off, and even better he was very talented and I would look good bathed in his afterglow.

CDP was the world's cleverest and most provocative agency in those days, that specialized in ads that actually had the public looking forward to commercial breaks. I was very lucky to get into CDP in 1966, on the coat-tails of working with Ross Cramer as an art director/copywriter team. CDP's creative director didn't really care about me, but he wanted Ross very much, and reluctantly ended up with young Saatchi as part of the package.

The creative director was the dour and reticent Colin Millward, as close to an advertising genius that Britain would produce, and with a magnificent North Country accent. He dismissed my copywriting efforts as piss-poor, but patiently helped me get better, in what became a delightful relationship.

Fortunately for me I also found an ally in David Puttnam, a young account manager who at the time was a super-cool Paul McCartney lookalikee, who sold my campaigns to some high profile clients, which did me no harm at all. As David wrote in Colin Millward's obituary in 2004 all the best creative people in advertising learnt it all from Colin, and even learnt that if you didn't really have a decent idea, give the commercial to Ridley Scott and he would turn a brainless 30 seconds into something exotic and widely admired. Colin also knew that if you wanted some gentle English humour and a nice play-on-words in the headline ('When it rains it shines' for Ford's new super-glossy paint finish), you would go to my next door neighbour down CDP's corridor, Alan Parker. And if you wanted something basic and crude you would come to me and hope for the best.

David Puttnam went on to win an Oscar for Best Picture with *Chariots of Fire* and is now Lord Puttnam. Ridley Scott went on to make *Alien, Blade Runner, Thelma & Louise, Gladiator, American Gangster* and *Hannibal.* He became Sir Ridley Scott in 2003. Alan Parker went on to make *Bugsy Malone, The Commitments, Mississippi Burning, Midnight Express* and *Evita.* He became Sir Alan Parker in 2002.

I am incapable of humility, so please believe me when I report that the only skill I possessed was to string together a few decent ideas a year, and occasionally these advertisements appeared to work quite well for our clients.

When I started the Saatchi & Saatchi agency with my brother, we were still in our early twenties, and it's hard to imagine how any client could entrust their advertising account to two pushy youths with silly names, carrying-on with a burning righteousness that would have fooled nobody.

Or so one would think.

There is no answer or formula I can offer. We worked brutally hard, and got blindingly lucky to get it to grow to be the world's biggest.

My brother did the client contact part, and we made sure he was so well briefed, so well versed, that whenever he attended a meeting with head people from prospective clients, he knew more about the client's problems and opportunities, and more about their competitor's prospects and weaknesses than any other person sat there.

Not much different to the Method School of Acting where you "become" the part you are playing, Stanislavski style. We adopted the Method approach so my brother could "become" a purposeful executive, vital and energetic, alert to new ways of improving your business model and build your brands, bursting with flair and optimism.

However laughable this must sound, for some reason it worked. Of course, it didn't hurt that my brother was well-endowed in the brains and charm dept, certainly more than I was.

At our agency, the trainee schemes were usually filled with Oxford and Cambridge graduates who went on to become management executives. But I, of course, enjoyed watching young hopeful copywriters who walked into reception with no training or experience and managed to talk their way into a trial couple of days to show what they could do. One in ten of our highest paid writers were walk-ins, and an equal percentage of the agency's key managers were school dropouts with no academic skills but quick-witted brains.

If you have a son or daughter who likes the idea of having fun and being paid exceptionally well while doing it, advertising is ideal, whether they have a double first from Oxford, or are an academic failure, shelf-stacking at Sainsburys. As long as they are not totally dim at everything, my best advice would be for them to not give up until they get a foot in the door at a top twenty ad agency in London or New York.

You should advise them to start off by finding out about each specialist department within an agency, because they each need differing skills, and personalities. Choose the bits that sound right and apply for a graduate traineeship. If they can't get one of those, tell them to take anything that will get them inside. Did I mention, they mustn't give up until they've got a foot in the door at a top twenty ad agency?

Whatever small abilities you have can be put to good use somewhere in an ad agency, whether it's your charm and wit for client hand-holding, technical talents suited to the complex world of media buying, or if you must, writing slogans and soundbites for power-hungry politicians.

It's a lovely life full of entertaining people and a thrill-a-minute atmosphere. And if you're good, the pay is high even while you're young enough to spend it madly.

What I adored most about our advertising agency was the fanatical devotion to keeping our clients happy, our desperate longing to have our campaigns succeed for them, and to win as many big accounts as possible.

We were maniacally driven to impress our clientele, and if all other businesses cared as much about providing satisfaction as ad agencies, we would have no need for automated Customer Service Helplines everywhere.

Beethoven Composing, Carl Schlösser, c.1890

LUCKY FOR ME, THERE'S NO JUSTICE IN THIS WORLD.

Expecting the world to treat you fairly because you are good, is like expecting the bull not to charge because you are a vegetarian.

Are you careful to put other people first? Are you anxious about other people's happiness and well-being?

Are you a caring listener and a reliable friend? Are you a sensitive and considerate person?

If you have answered yes to any of the above, I believe we have pinpointed your first mistake. Unlock yourself from the neurotic need to please. It erodes the soul. You will forever feel not quite good enough. Your worthiness becomes so expected, inevitably your defects become too easily seized upon, and indeed magnified. Everybody is needy, arrogant, callous, aggrieved, self-absorbed, petty, mean-spirited, spiteful, greedy, envious, ill-mannered and malicious, in some measure, some of the time.

Only when you accept that much of the pleasure of being alive is to enjoy your own horribleness, and the character flaws in everyone around you, will you find harmony and each day will pass more sweetly.

Mahatma Gandhi was very keen on justice, and as he eloquently observed on vengefulness, "An eye for an eye would leave the whole world blind."

If the Mahatma had only given me a call before delivering this observation, I would have been happy to set him straight. "An eye for an eye" isn't a demand for barbaric retribution. It was a liberal and measured call demanding that punishment should be proportionate, and fit the crime, e.g. you don't chop off someone's head just for stealing a horse.

As for revenge, of course it is deeply pleasurable. But it can come about in many forms. Nobody likes burglars, muggers and fraudsters but theirs is a career choice and they are presumably prepared to be incarcerated for their actions if by some small chance they are caught.

We can find a small grain of comfort in the certainty that unpleasant thieves usually end up leading miserable lives, even if they actually believe it will be just lovely living in the Spanish Riviera on the proceeds of their crimes. Wouldn't you rather have passed away than exist in the Costa del Sol surrounded by the cream of South London gangbangers, with endless rounds of golf and sangria, eating tapas and paella, and going lobster red in the blistering heat, in the company of other unsavoury psychopathic dullards?

Everyone would agree that before you begin a journey of revenge, dig two graves, one for yourself. Everyone would also tell you that you cannot get ahead while you are getting even. All I would ask myself is – would I bite a dog because the dog bit me? In those circumstances, revenge can truly turn you rabid.

I do not believe in fate. I do not believe your destiny is controlled by you. I do not believe that you can command the outcome of your life. People are tossed about in a capricious sea of unknowable, indiscriminate circumstances. Some drown. Some survive. Some thrive.

Beethoven's confrontation with fate and destiny is a good example of our ongoing battle with these forces beyond our control. Physically and emotionally abused as a boy, he was extremely introverted as a child and became increasingly isolated from the world as a young man, frustrated by his efforts to earn a living as a musician.

Then, at the age of twenty-eight, just as his music was starting to attract attention, he began to lose his hearing. His first reaction was anger, followed by a deep depression. "The most beautiful years of my life must pass without accomplishing the promise of my talent and powers," he wrote to a close friend.

But six months later, Beethoven had decided "to take Fate by the throat; it shall not wholly overcome me", even though he was profoundly deaf by the age of 45, twelve years before his death. It was during this period that he composed his greatest music including the Missa Solemnis, the Ninth Symphony, six string quartets and his final piano sonatas.

Beethoven accepted his fate but he refused to allow it to determine his destiny.

Sadly, almost none of us possesses both Beethoven's genius and will, and can do little more than flail about in our sea of circumstance.

For what it's worth, I think that if you cannot find happiness because you are constantly overwhelmed by the relative misfortune of others, then you are simply not sufficiently grateful for your own good fortune. As an example, it doesn't help the homeless feel any better knowing that people with a roof over their heads don't fully appreciate it.

In general, everybody finds people more cynical and mistrusting these days. But then, most of our suspicions of others are aroused by our knowledge of ourselves.

I am keenly aware that in my own fortuitous life, justice is as blind to my flaws and vileness as it is to your humility and virtue.

Whenever I feel guilt-wracked by the providential existence I have been granted, I always take myself off to see a good disaster movie.

But could we discuss a movie that in itself was truly a disaster?

Pulgasari is a North Korean film produced in 1985, with a *Godzilla*-esque monster rampaging crossly around Korea in 1200 AD, as its central plot line. What roused interest in this epic was that it was produced by a South Korean director Shin Sang-ok, who had been kidnapped seven years earlier by North Korean Intelligence, on the orders of Kim Jong-il, son of the then ruler Kim Il-sung.

Japan's Toho Studio, creators of the original *Godzilla*, participated in *Pulgasari's* special effects; a doll comes to life when a child pricks her finger, and the drop of blood on the doll creates our Hero who starts eating all the iron it can find, growing bigger and glowing with intense heat.

Apparently, critics at the time suggested that the film was intended as a propaganda metaphor – unchecked capitalism being overcome by the power of the collective - so you certainly don't want to miss it.

Disaster movies have embraced:

Avalanches – *Avalanche Express* 1979	Earthquakes – *San Francisco* 1936
Comets – *Deep Impact* 1998	Asteroids – *Armageddon* 1998
Volcanoes – *Krakatoa, East of Java* 1969	Floods – *Flood* 2007
Tsunami – *Tidal Wave* 2009	Fires – *The Towering Inferno* 1974
Epidemics – *Outbreak* 1995	Aliens – *War of the Worlds* 2005
Chemicals – *The Crazies* 2010	Ships – *The Poseidon Adventure* 1972
Theme parks – *Rollercoaster* 1977	Trains – *Unstoppable* 2010
Insects – *Arachnophobia* 1990	Tornadoes – *Twister* 1996
Plants – *Day of the Triffids* 1972	Monsters – *Cloverfield* 2008
Nuclear energy – *The Sum of All Fears* 2002	Climate – *The Day After Tomorrow* 2004

Few of these were not entirely disastrous.

The world remains horrified by the Tsunami catastrophe of 2004, probably because we were largely unaware that such a natural phenomenon could occur. I couldn't stop myself researching other calamities that were out of the ordinary e.g. not earthquakes, volcanic eruptions, whirlwinds, hurricanes and the like.

That's how I heard about The Boston Molasses (or treacle as it is known in Britain) Disaster, or The Great Molasses Flood. It occurred in 1919, when a molasses storage tank, 50ft tall and 90ft in diameter containing 2,300 gallons, burst. A wave of the treacle rushed through the streets at an estimated 35mph, at a height of 12ft, killing 21 and injuring 150.

Witnesses stated there was a sound like machine-gun fire as the rivets shot out of the tank, before it collapsed. Buildings were swept off their foundations, and the girders of the adjacent elevated railway structure were snapped. Horses and other animals were among the victims, and coughing fits were commonplace for months after amongst the local population.

The tank was never rebuilt and the site is currently a city-owned baseball field. Not on a par with the horror of the Tsunami of course, but alarming nonetheless if you were in the North end of Boston at the time.

I also stumbled upon two particularly unusual ways to die. One of the more pleasant exits would be to emulate Alex Mitchell, a 50 year old from Norfolk, England who died in 1975 whilst watching *The Goodies* on TV. A particular scene had caused Mitchell to laugh non-stop for twenty-five minutes before dying from heart failure; a puzzlingly bizarre death, as *The Goodies* is possibly the unfunniest TV comedy ever made.

I wouldn't care to echo the demise of Gregory Biggs, from Fort Worth, Texas, who in 2001 was struck by a car driven by Chante Mallard and became lodged in her windscreen, with severe but not immediately fatal injuries. Mallard drove home and left the car in her garage with Biggs still trapped on the car; he died of his injuries several hours later.

But if you like the picturesque, you are free to emulate Kenneth Pinyan of Gig Harbour, Washington, who died in 2005 of acute peritonitis after receiving anal intercourse from a stallion, leading to the criminalization of bestiality in Washington State.

I enjoy a tale of providential death, of course, assuming it was such a long time ago, your schadenfreude doesn't feel unseemly.

In 620 BC, Draco, the 'draconian' lawmaker in ancient Athens, was smothered to death by cloaks showered on him by appreciative citizens at a theatre in Aegina.

In 892, Sigurd the Mighty strapped the head of his defeated foe, Mael Brigte, to his horse's saddle. The teeth of the severed head grazed against his leg repeatedly as he rode, causing a fatal, and indeed mighty, infection.

Bela I of Hungary died in 1063 when the magnificent, jewel encrusted canopy above his throne collapsed upon him.

In 1667 James Betts was hidden in a cupboard by his lover Elizabeth Spencer, who didn't want her dad to find him in her bedroom. The unfortunate Betts died of asphyxiation.

Poor Molière, the French playwright and actor, died after being seized by a violent coughing fit, whilst playing the title role in his play *The Hypochondriac*.

But, he always did have a thing about irony.

Voilà

BEING THICK IS NO OBSTACLE TO BEING A SUCCESSFUL ARTIST.

I admire all artists. It's the cruellest job you could take on, particularly if you are gifted, but forever unrecognized. But by and large talent is in such short supply, mediocrity can be taken for brilliance rather more than genius can go undiscovered.

People inspecting the art world mutter about artists getting as rich as Damien Hirst, a millionaire 100 times over. But if you think of art as entertainment, his pay-scale sits alongside Tiger Woods, George Clooney, Roger Federer, Johnny Depp, Madonna and the other superstars.

If you prefer to think of art as something more spiritual, and disapprove, can we agree that there is something very spiritual about Roger Federer's backhand?

Art only flourished in the Renaissance because it was subsidized by the rich, and the Church. Even sacred art relied on patronage and successful artists who were in demand became wealthy. Perhaps even in those days people were more fascinated by how much art fetched, than the art itself.

In today's faux-fame culture, better to be a celebrity because people talk about your art, rather than your wedding photos in *Hello!*

And there is nothing new about artists seeking attention, even notoriety, by producing provocative work.

Théodore Géricault was a young painter who wanted to create work that generated wide public interest. At the time, major large-scale works were commissioned, but Géricault decided to create a depiction of an infamous event in 1816, as an independent undertaking. He created a vast painting, *The Raft of the Medusa*, measuring 491 x 716 cm, depicting the aftermath of the French frigate *Méduse* running aground off Mauritania. 147 people were set adrift on a hurriedly constructed raft; all but 15 died in the 13 days before their rescue, and survivors endured starvation, dehydration, cannibalism and madness.

The story fired up Géricault's imagination and ambition, and he undertook extensive research, interviewing two of the survivors, and visiting the morgues and hospitals where he could view first-hand the colour and texture of the dying and the dead.

The painting caused the desired effect when it was shown for the first time at the 1819 Paris Salon, attracting a storm of controversy, praise and condemnation in equal measure.

Though it retains the traditions of history painting, it represented a crucial break from the calm and order of the then prevailing Neoclassical school, and is now seen as seminal in the formation of the Romantic Movement in French painting.

Today, hanging in the Louvre it is still a startling work, its overwhelming presence staying with every viewer forever.

And it is still possible, even today, to make an ambitious large-scale work that creates headlines, controversy, and strong opinions from supporters and detractors alike: Marcus Harvey's portrait of child murderer Myra Hindley created using children's handprints.

Of course, not all successful artists are more intelligent than other people. I have always been hesitant about visiting artists' studios, and discovering that work I have admired has been made by someone nitwitted. This can be disconcerting if you believe an artist paints with his brains, not with his hands.

But if you study a great work of art, you'll probably find the artist was a kind of genius. And geniuses are different to you and me. So let's have no talk of temperamental, self-absorbed and petulant babies. It's a tough career to make a success of, you have to be a little nuts to take it on, and it helps that you clearly have no need to be particularly bright.

And I am testimony to the fact that you can be thick as a brick and buy art all day long. With a collecting obsessive/compulsive disorder, my aim in life is not so much the pursuit of happiness, rather the happiness of pursuit.

I can offer you a foolproof method to become a successful sculptor.

If you have absolutely no artistic training whatsoever, sculpt an elephant. First, get an immense block of marble the size of a bus or coach. Then chip away anything that doesn't look like an elephant.

Voilà. An imposing, possibly abstract work, that would be snapped up to be placed outside a corporate headquarters or within the grand lobby, and attract much attention and wonder.

I bought a more professional piece of sculpture today, a wooden creation by a young artist, Dmitri Galitzine. He carved Benson, Britain's biggest and most loved carp according to *Angler's Mail* in 2005.

Benson was female, one of a pair, but her partner Hedges disappeared in a flood in 1998. They were named after the cigarette brand, because Benson had a hole in her dorsal fin resembling a cigarette burn.

At the time of her death in July 2009, she weighted the same as a large dog, and had been caught 63 times in 13 years. She was 25 and had lived at the Kingfisher Lake outside Oundle in Cambridgeshire. I don't have the slightest interest in fishing, but rather liked the sculpture.

Outdoor sculpture is an important component of the art world, but considering it is seen by more of the public than any other kind of art, it gets comparatively little critical attention.

Personally, I find public sculpture rather fascinating.

If you see a statue of a man on a horse, and the horse has both its front legs in the air – the man died in battle. If the horse has one leg in the air, the rider died later, but as a result of wounds received in battle. If the horse has all four legs on the ground, the rider died of natural causes.

I did actually believe these helpful guidelines to municipal artworks until I saw the monument with Washington's horse holding one paw in the air, despite its rider dying of natural causes. In general, however, most public sculpture is fairly dismal because it will have been approved by committee, and committees rarely make aesthetic breakthroughs in the works they commission.

And art is often seen as a blight by residents living with a big sculpture on their doorstep. The locals are often vocal in their complaints, as they were once about a Richard Serra installation in New York.

In truth, although I greatly admire Richard Serra, I don't know that I would want a 100ft long 10ft tall steel wall perched in the gardens outside my home. After a while, I fear I might miss the views of the flowers and trees.

As I am clearly seen as someone with an immense ego, some wag asked me if I was planning a portrait or death mask of myself to exhibit in my gallery for posterity.

It was a charming notion, which I have inexplicably overlooked.

I was always intrigued by the 'Unknown Woman of the Seine' whose death mask became a familiar sight in a number of artists' homes after 1900. The body of a young woman was pulled out of the river at the Quai du Louvre in Paris in 1888.

Her corpse showed no signs of violence, and suicide was suspected. A pathologist at the Paris morgue was so struck by her beauty, that he created a plaster cast of her face, and in later years, numerous copies were produced.

They became a fashionable but morbid decoration in Parisian bohemian life: Albert Camus compared her enigmatic smile to that of the *Mona Lisa*, inviting much speculation about what clues the eerily cheerful expression on her face signified about her life, her death and her position in society.

Al Alvarez wrote in his book on suicide *The Savage God*, that a generation of German girls modelled themselves on her. The 'L'Inconnue de la Seine' became the erotic ideal of the period, as Bardot was for the 1950s. Greta Garbo's icy allure and aloofness is also thought to have been inspired by the haunting features.

I do hope my own death mask is as captivating over the coming decades.

London has some remarkable outdoor sculpture. I very much like the statue of Winston Churchill by Ivor Roberts-Jones in Parliament Square, but that's probably because I like Churchill so much.

Did you know that embedded above Sotheby's entrance is the oldest outdoor statue in London? The Ancient Egyptian black basalt effigy of the lion-goddess Sekhmet, dates to around 1320 BC. It has been Sotheby's muse since the 1880s when it was sold at auction for £40 but never collected by the buyer.

Nearby, four abstract pieces by Henry Moore adorn the Time-Life Building off Bond Street. He had carved them in his garden in 1953, and once they were in place, he asked to buy them back, as he thought the third floor was too high for them to be seen properly. He was right.

People often think that to be a successful artist, first you must be prepared to be self-critical. Self-critique is a fine notion in theory, but nothing changes the fact that some days you are the pigeon, and some days the statue.

LOBBYING FOR BEGINNERS.

Before we opened the Saatchi & Saatchi agency, we recognized the value of an imposing lobby.

When we started out our lobby was bigger than our offices, but we had such few staff it didn't matter. We used to hire people off the street to man the typewriters and click away busily whenever a prospective client walked through, creating an atmosphere that was thrusting and vibrant. Embarrassing to admit this ridiculousness, but it was so long ago…

I was never able to resuscitate my reputation after rumours spread about me dressing up as a cleaner, so that I could avoid meeting a client. There was no dressing up. I was a touch shy in the early days about meeting clientele, and did once use my hanky to clean the handrails, head down giving them a thorough polish, to shrink from a client walking through.

I regret it obviously, because when that little tidbit of gossip circulated, my reputation as being somewhat creepy, possibly certifiable, became fixed solid. Happily people quickly accepted that I was a back-room boy best kept far away from clients, which suited me just fine.

As our agency grew, our lobbies grew ever larger, as did the rumours of what was happening inside the building. Though I have only ever had one puff of a marijuana cigarette, I don't much care if other people smoke them until they're cross-eyed. But I was alarmed when my agency began being widely referred to as White City.

Although many of our people were very hyper, worked 20-hour days fuelled by something other than enthusiasm, queues of odd-looking people were making deliveries at all hours, and some of our execs' mood swings and paranoia were alarming, the clients seemed happy enough, the creative work was ok and sometimes brilliant, staff morale extraordinarily high, and the business just kept on growing and growing.

I didn't ever feel the need to take any moral high ground, but more importantly didn't want to appear wet and already prissy and past it before I hit 35.

Behind the foolishly large lobbies, we did need to produce advertising campaigns that occasionally worked, to maintain a reputation as credible firebrands of the industry.

I heard a little parable as a youth that inspired me to accept that a good piece of ad copy could make the difference between a dull message and a compelling one.

An elderly blind man was seated on the pavement on a busy street, begging for small change from passers-by. Next to his collection plate, he had erected a cardboard sign "Blind – please help". Very few pedestrians were paying him any attention.

An advertising writer walking by saw the empty collection plate, and noticed that people were completely unmoved, with almost nobody dropping in any money. The writer took a marker-pen from his pocket, turned the cardboard sheet around, and wrote a new message on the back. Soon the collection plate was overflowing.

The blind man asked the stranger to tell him what the sign now said. "It says" answered the stranger, "It's a beautiful day. You can see it. I cannot."

Of course, some people claim a good ad man could sell a refrigerator to an Eskimo. They forget that people regularly sell refrigerators to Eskimos, where they keep their food from freezing.

These days, either I've changed or the advertising industry has, but I simply loathe commercials interrupting programmes.

Of course, when I was making commercials I always hated the silly way programmes kept interrupting our ads. But hand-on-heart I do think ads today are corny, the ad breaks are interminably longer and more frequent than they used to be, and the broadcasters raise the volume to piercing levels during advertisements to arrest your attention.

All very irritating and self-destructive because, as you point out, many people now have the technology to zip past the commercial breaks, and so of course they do. And if they don't, the commercial breaks are now so lengthy, they have time to create a 3-course meal rather than the traditional cup of tea. The stupidity of advertisers and broadcasters who take the public a) for granted and b) for mugs is bewildering. Being greedy and short-sighted is one thing. But pretending the internet isn't around and taking over your world is another.

Of course, my background in advertising has delighted art commentators, and it has proven to be an enduring and highly appealing demonstration of the 'adman' shallowness of the kind of art I favour.

But the snobbery of those who think an interest in art is the province of gentle souls of rarefied sensibility never fails to entertain. Lord forbid that anyone in 'trade' should enter the hallowed portals of the cognoscenti.

Please feel safe to assume that in both the art world and the advertising world there are an equal number of bumptious charlatans and cultivated aesthetes.

I liked working in advertising, but don't believe my taste in art, such as it is, was entirely formed by TV commercials. And I don't feel especially conflicted enjoying a Mantegna one day, a Carl Andre the next day and a student work the next.

Unlike many of the art world heavy hitters and deep thinkers, I don't believe painting is middle-class and bourgeois, incapable of saying anything meaningful anymore, too impotent to hold much sway.

For me, and for people with good eyes who actually enjoy looking at art, nothing is as uplifting as standing before a great painting, whether it was painted in 1505 or last Tuesday.

The Cardsharps (I Bari), Caravaggio, c.1594 (detail)

THE POORER YOU ARE AT POKER, THE RICHER YOU ARE IN FRIENDS.

I am laughably inept at poker. Indeed I am always in demand at various poker games because I am a predictably reliable loser. Poker requires, amongst other skills, patience. Good players are prepared to sit out many hands if their initial cards aren't promising. I am foolish enough to be intoxicated by the prospects of almost any opening cards I am dealt, and I continue to bet until my doom becomes all too clear.

I'm not sure that great poker players are always particularly lovely people. Being the best they can be is often costly in the congeniality dept., particularly when their obsession borders upon a compulsive disorder.

A friend, worried about his lack of a poker face or a 'tell' in his facial expressions was so driven by his concern about the readability of his outward giveaways, that he had a multiple course of Botox fillers in a misguided attempt to eradicate any visual reactions whatsoever to the strength or weakness of his cards. He even considered if he could be surgically infected with Möbius Syndrome, a rare neurological disorder characterized by facial paralysis.

We had to talk him down from this fixation to achieve a perfect 'dead face' to confound his poker opponents. I know I sounded like his mum, but I persuaded him that when he stumbled across other pleasures in life away from the poker table, it might prove confusing being unable to smile.

I am also hopelessly weak at chess and abandoned playing altogether when I read a report from Moscow of an alarming death of a chess player whose brain exploded, literally, in the middle of a championship game.

No one else was hurt in the fatal eruption, but four players and three officials at the Moscow Candidate Masters Chess Challenge were sprayed with blood and brain matter when Nicolai Titov's head suddenly blew apart. "He was deep in concentration with his eyes focused on the board", said Titov's opponent Vladimir Dobrynin, "then all of a sudden his hands flew to his temples, he screamed in pain, as if someone had placed a bomb in his head, and it exploded."

Doctors blamed an extremely rare electrical imbalance, Hyper Cerebral Disorder, but I'm taking no chances and giving up my quest for Grandmaster, and am better suited to the skill required for scratch cards.

I can beat weaker players than me at Scrabble. I spent many hours learning all the bizarre 2 and 3 letter words in the Scrabble dictionary, pages of obscure anagrams, instantly wasted when they changed the dictionary to be used in championships. They've recently changed it again for the online version, so virtually any letter combination you can imagine now seems to be ok, he whimpered bitterly.

Besides, the world champions all come from Thailand or Korea, can barely speak a word of English, but have committed the entire Chambers and Oxford Dictionaries to memory, and see the game as a mathematical challenge retrieving their built-in superchip listings.

In the UK, we do have a world class player in Mikki Nicholson, 32 yrs, a transsexual who was anointed UK National Champion in November 2010, in a pink wig and matching PVC dress. She took the crown with "obeisant" which scored 86 points.

The recreational activity I enjoy the most is settling down to Match of the Day, the week's TV highlight in our house. It's Gary Lineker's, Alan Hansen's and Mark Lawrenson's shirts on Match of the Day that make it so compelling, besides the occasional decent game. Every week they each produce their latest find, with delightful stripes, lovely piping and cuff details, and an exotic array of collar styles. That, and the punditry and commentary:

"Denied" as in "denied by the woodwork", a goal stopped by the goal posts.

"Clash"/"scrap" the top four premiership teams playing each other clash, the bottom four scrap.

"Attentions" a defender's efforts at hounding his opponent for the ball.

"Calling card" a player's delivery of a heavy challenge, flooring an opponent.

"Cauldron" a heated atmosphere.

"Cynical foul" when the player committing it doesn't even pretend it's an accident.

"Drought" no goals again, from a team with a run of poor results.

"Twelfth man" enthusiastic and supportive spectators.

"Screamer" a player "lets fly" with a powerful strike (sorry, kick).

"Fortress" a well-defended goal area, as in "they park the team bus" in the goal mouth.

"Ghost" a player who flits quietly around the opposition, unmarked.

"Hairdryer" a severe and noisy telling off at close range by the manager.

"Sitter" an easy goal chance, often missed/squandered.

"Handbags" a disagreement between players, where nobody is actually punched senseless.

"In their faces" a team that quickly and aggressively closes down any opposition move.

"Metatarsal" a part of the foot we are now all familiar with because it is regularly a victim of injury.

"Pub team" an amateur, lacklustre performance.

"Service" a neat and accurate pass from the midfield to the forwards.

"Silverware" are trophies.

"Talismanic" an inspiring player who can affect the outcome of a match.

"Tap up" an illegal approach to try and secure the services of another team's player.

"Big ask" when a minnow team need to beat Man U 4-0 to fend-off relegation.

"Torrid time" the lot of a player regularly made to look slow and clumsy by the forward he's trying to mark.

"Warming the bench" are players sitting on the sideline as potential substitutes.

"Aristocrats" are the ten biggest teams in European football.

"Anonymous" a player who has had a lacklustre game and made little impact.

"Clinical" a neatly executed goal.

"Group of death" when England are drawn into a qualifying shortlist that includes decent opposition.

Best of all, to the delight of Harry Enfield and Paul Whitehouse, those unmissable post-match player interviews with the incomprehensible Portuguese, Scottish or Croatian accents, and the managers with their distinctive facial tics, verbal dysfunctions and greasy comb-overs.

Note: Poker graphically illustrates the wisdom of Gore Vidal's observation: It isn't enough to succeed, other's must fail – and that money won is twice as sweet as money earned. I learnt very early in my poker playing days that if after the first twenty minutes you don't know who the sucker at the table is, it's you.

Sylvester Agoglia, Charles 'Lucky' Luciano, and Meyer Lansky

I MISS THE MAFIA.

The Mafia has a special place in the hearts of everyone who loved *The Godfather* movies.

Is there anything more glamorous than the world of Mafia mobsters, the ruthless power battles between the crime families, the code of Omertà where members are sworn to keep schtum, the symbolic messages of dead fish that were delivered as a warning to keep in line, or horse's heads placed in your bed, or a canary left strangled and dangled on your porch, or worse, on your corpse?

I am sure we are all a mite saddened that the FBI and the Italian Police have become too efficient at locking up Mafiosi.

In 2007, Sicilian police managed to arrest Salvatore Lo Piccolo, the reputed boss of bosses of Cosa Nostra based on the island, after many years of trying to nail him. In their search of Salvatore's house, they found an intriguing document he had drawn up, a charter to being a member of good standing in the Mafia family. Amongst the papers were details of corporations with Mafia connections, and information about the hierarchy within the crime families, all of which were heavily coded.

When the code was broken, so were several other members of the Mafia fiefdoms. Salvatore's charter, or the Mafia's Ten Commandments that he had created reads as follows:

1. No-one can present himself directly to another of our friends. There must be a third person to do it.

2. Never look at the wives of family members or friends.

3. Never be seen with cops.

4. Don't go to bars or clubs.

5. Always being available for Cosa Nostra is a duty – even if your wife's about to give birth.

6. Appointments must absolutely be respected.

7. Wives must be treated with courtesy.

8. When asked for information by the family, the answer must always be the truth.

9. Money cannot be appropriated if it belongs to others in the family, or to other families.

10. People who can't be part of Cosa Nostra: anyone who has a close relative in the police, anyone with a two-timing relative in their family, anyone who behaves badly and doesn't hold to moral values.

To become a member of the Cosa Nostra – a man of honour, or a 'made man', you don't ask to join, you are invited. You will have been watched carefully for a couple of years, after an existing member has put your name forward; this is itself a hazardous business as your supporter will be held responsible for a bad choice, with dire consequences.

Joe Valachi, who quickly rose through the ranks, was swayed into joining up by Mafioso Bobby Doyle, who explained that a solo career of crime, was much more dangerous than being 'made.'

For Joe Valachi, the baptizing ceremony involved Joe Bonanno slicing his finger with a dagger, the blood dripping onto the image of a saint, which was then burnt.

He then was sworn-in on the understanding that if he disobeyed the rules, 'his flesh would burn like the saint.'

Of course, Joe Valachi was the prime source in 1963 of evidence that led to the FBI's first breakthrough in weakening the stronghold of the Families.

The Mafia was often described as a cartel of 'security' firms, that protected 'customers' who paid up to eradicate problems with thieves, or competitors, or anyone trying to cheat them.

Clients included landowners, politicians, shopkeepers, drug dealers, loan sharks, smugglers, pimps and trades unions.

The Mafia grew rich and powerful as heavily paid enforcers, and were widely feared because they were merciless about murdering anyone who interfered with the smooth running of their affairs, even amongst their own.

In 1980 Philadelphia Mafia Consigliere Antonio Caponigro had Angelo Bruno killed without approval of the heads of the ruling Families.

Caponigro was found suffocated, beaten, stabbed, shot three times behind the right ear and once behind the left ear and had cash stuffed up his rectum as a sign that he had become too greedy.

In Sicily, nearly 70% of all businesses pay protection to the Mafia Families, bringing in €10 million annually from that source alone.

But the days of Mafia glory have been eroded by the weight of drug escalation.

The enormous proceeds from narcotics have enabled the Black, Columbian and Hispanic crime syndicates to sideline the Mafia to a degree that you, I, and the FBI cannot welcome; we look back nostalgically at the calmer days of monopoly held by the Cosa Nostra families and their more upright Code of Honour.

Can we raise a glass to our favourite Mafia bosses Salvatore 'Lucky' Luciano, head of the Genovese crime family, Benjamin 'Bugsy' Siegel, one of the founding members of 'Murder, Inc.', Frank Costello head of the Luciano family (Marlon Brando imitated Costello's raspy voice in the role of Don Corleone), Albert Anastasia, head of the Gambino family, Vincenzo 'The Chin' Gigante, who made the Genovese family the most powerful in the US under his leadership.

Salute per favore.

Calvin Graham, was the youngest U.S. serviceman, during World War II. Following the attack on Pearl Harbor, he enlisted in the Navy in May 1942, at the age of 12

WAR DOESN'T DETERMINE WHO'S RIGHT, WAR DETERMINES WHO'S LEFT.

Pacifists who have taken this stance are not misguided or naïve. Nobody celebrates the savagery that war inflicts on innocent civilians, or the vileness of young troops risking their lives or their limbs.

But isn't it being blithely sentimental to overlook wars that are unavoidable – to right a wrong, to save more lives than are lost, to create a more secure and happier future for coming generations?

I am completely delighted that I have never had to participate on a battlefield, and would have sobbed into my pillow all night at the prospect of facing an infantry assault the following morning.

However, I can fantasise about being a real man, like Simo Häyhä, a Finnish farmer, who served his mandatory year in the military, but decided to lay down his milking buckets and pick up his trusty rifle to help his homeland, when the Soviet army invaded in 1939.

Since the majority of the fighting took place in the forest, he decided the best way to stop the invasion was to hide in a tree with some cans of food, shooting Russians.

It was 20-40 degrees below zero, with a six foot deep carpet of snow. When the Russians heard that dozens of their men were going down, and that it was just one man with a rifle, he became known as 'The White Death' because of his white camouflage outfit, and they mounted entire missions to finish him off.

When the first task force located him, he killed them all. Then the Russians tried putting together a team of counter-snipers to root him out. He killed them all too. Over the course of 100 days, Häyhä killed 542 soldiers with his rifle. He took out another 163 with his sub-machine gun, sending his tally to 705. Since by now everyone was too dead or too scared to go anywhere near him, the Russians just carpet-bombed everywhere they thought he might be. He got hit by a cloud of shrapnel, that tore his coat up, but didn't actually injure him.

Finally, on March 6th 1940, someone managed to shoot Häyhä in the head with an exploding bullet. When other soldiers found him, he was brought back to base with half his head missing. 'The White Death' had finally been stopped… for about a week. He regained consciousness on March 13th, the day the war ended, and lived happily ever after until 1st April 2002.

Battle has also brought out the extraordinary in many other people. Calvin Graham was 12 years old when he enlisted in the U.S. Navy after the attack on Pearl Harbor. He was wounded in combat and given a Dishonourable Discharge for lying about his age – though his benefits were later restored by public demand and an Act of Congress.

The Russians destroyed over 500 German aircraft by ramming their own planes into them in midair, and also cleared minefields by marching over them. As Joseph Stalin pointed out 'It takes a brave man not to be a hero in the Red Army'.

One of Japan's most effective methods of destroying tanks was to bury a large artillery shell, with only the nose exposed. When a tank approached a Japanese soldier half-buried next to the shell, jumped up, hammered the shell, destroying the tank and himself. 'Lack of correct weapons is no excuse for defeat' was the policy of Lt. General Mataguchi.

At a more prosaic level, we should feel proud that when the U.S. Army landed in North Africa, amongst its priorities was the installation of three complete Coca-Cola bottling plants.

Have you ever read about the longest war on record – the Three Hundred and Fifty Years War, between the Netherlands and the Isles of Scilly off the Southwest coast of Britain, which was finally declared over in 1986.

It is certainly the war with the fewest casualties, without a single shot being fired. You can blame it all on Oliver Cromwell, who forced the Royalists to retreat off the Cornish coast to Scilly.

The Dutch had sought to ally with whoever emerged as the victorious side in the Second English Civil war, but when the Royalists inflicted heavy losses on the Dutch fleet based in Scilly, the Netherlands demanded reparations, and when none were forthcoming, declared war.

But as by now England was in Parliamentarian hands, the war was declared specifically on the Isles of Scilly.

Peace wasn't declared until a historian, and chairman of the Scilly council, invited the Dutch Ambassador to sign a peace treaty in April 1986.

Ambassador Rein Huydecoper, the wag, joked that "it must have been harrowing living on Scilly and knowing the Dutch could have attacked at any moment."

In the endless list of futile conflict over the years, the War of the Stray Dog takes some beating as the world's most foolish. A Greek soldier ran after his dog which had wandered across the border with Bulgaria, on October 22nd 1925, near the town of Petrich. Bulgarian border sentries shot him instantly, and fatally.

In a tense political climate, Greek General Pangalos sent a military unit into Bulgaria and attempted to occupy Petrich. He demanded punishment of the Bulgarian commander of the troops that had shot his man, and an official government apology to Greece, and six million Drachma as compensation for the soldier's family.

Although Bulgarian troops provided only token resistance, trusting the League of Nations to settle the dispute, volunteers from the whole region rushed to defend Petrich, and before the League had finally ruled, fifty were killed, mainly Bulgarian civilians. Greece acceded to pressure and withdrew. I have no idea if the dog survived.

More recently, everyone's favourite war story is the "unknown unknown".

I am fond of this little creation by US Secretary of Defence Donald Rumsfeld:

"There are known knowns; these are things we know we know. We also know there are known unknowns; that is to say we know there are some things we don't know. But there are also unknown unknowns – the ones we don't know we don't know."

He produced this insight at a press briefing in 2002, where he addressed the absence of evidence linking the government of Iraq with the supply of weapons of mass destruction to terrorist groups.

It was criticised at the time as an abuse of language by, amongst others, the Plain English Campaign.

However, I'm with linguist Geoffrey Pullum who said the quotation was "completely straightforward" and "impeccable syntactically, semantically, logically, and rhetorically".

I miss Donald Rumsfeld's little bits of homespun philosophy.

The army I was intrigued by was the Sacred Band of Thebes, a troop of handpicked soldiers consisting of 150 male couples. They formed the elite fighting corps of the Theban army in the 4th century BC.

The rationale for selecting male couples was that lovers would fight more fiercely and cohesively than a group of strangers formed together with no ardent bonds.

The 300 would stand in the brunt of the battle, and their skills as 'special forces' marked the 40 year prowess of Thebes as a military strength in early Greece, routing the Spartans in 375 BC, whose army was three times the size.

In 305 BC, the city of Thebes erected a monumental stone lion at the burial site of the Sacred Band, which was restored in the 20th century, and stands today as a pilgrimage destination for gay pride adherents.

I admit that I am very pleased not to have served in the military, though if circumstances, and my preferences, had been different the Sacred Band would have been an inspiring way to end my days.

Note: The fate that befell Lord Uxbridge after losing a limb was unpredictable. His leg was shattered by a cannon shot at the Battle of Waterloo in Belgium. His artificial leg had a peculiar after-life as a tourist attraction in the village of Waterloo in Belgium, where it had been interred, and it is now preserved at Plas Newydd in Anglesey. The saw used to amputate Lord Uxbridge's leg is held in the National Army Museum, London.

David Garrick and Mrs. Pritchard in "Macbeth", Johann Zoffany, 1768

IS THE THEATRE CLAPPED OUT?

I find the theatre faintly embarrassing for the actors performing on stage. It seems rather showy-off in an undignified way.

So although over the years I have seen dozens of plays that were entirely thrilling, mostly now, the moment the curtains open, I fall quickly asleep.

Of course, my poor wife finds this in itself faintly embarrassing, particularly when the lead or the playwright is a friend.

If it's a comedy, I always fear that people with little sense of humour laugh most easily. Just sit in a theatre during a play critics call 'screamingly funny' and as soon as the curtain opens and the lead steps on to the stage set, pours himself a glass of whisky and coughs, the audience starts guffawing. They are there to have a good time and their happy laughter mode is on full-beam. I, sadly, often find the entire experience 'screamingly dull' and sit barely managing a thin smile.

Theatre today simply doesn't have the same resonance that it did a century ago and certainly not following after the last sixty years of cinema and television.

My favourite theatrical memory is the exchange between George Bernard Shaw and Winston Churchill: "I am enclosing two tickets for the first night of my new play. Bring a friend... if you have one."

And Churchill's reply: "Can't possibly attend first night, will attend second... if there is one."

The contemporary playwrights I admire are Tom Stoppard and Simon Gray, but I prefer to read their plays rather than see them performed.

So despite the excellent reviews my performance as First Witch in *Macbeth* received in the school magazine, in a cutting I still carry that declared 'Saatchi illuminated the production', I fear that theatre is only very rarely able to compete for attention against the telly, which has the advantage in my house of being able to be viewed lying horizontal in bed.

Though I cannot adequately explain why it is called a TV set when you only get one, television has become the only logical place to watch films – I don't find sitting in the dark with a lot of strangers eating mammoth popcorn tubs and slurping litres of cola a great joy. If you place your handsome plasma set at the foot of the bed, with some decent speakers you get the full-on big screen experience, without the chatter of the people behind you, just the babble of your wife and children if it's a family-night-in.

I am not alone in arguing that the best of television is as good as the cream of the silver screen, usually with better scripts, sharper production and skilled directors. Everyone I know who works in television tells me that the BBC is run by Ed Poll, who few outside the organization will know, but who rules with an iron rod, turns the most hardened veteran producer into mush, micro-manages every detail of every production to bring each firmly into line, has a messianic belief in the critical importance of his work, and brooks no argument.

Ed Poll is Editorial Policy, which at the BBC goes beyond political correctness, and assumes the mantle of an Orwellian watcher, peering over all shoulders at all times within the BBC, to make absolutely certain that the Corporation output is blemish-free and not compromised in any way.

But, as the BBC allowed me to participate in the search for a new art star without having to put on make-up and actually appear on the show, I rather enjoyed being involved in a TV programme.

The truth is, I have been enormously grateful for the BBC my entire life, and without it Britain would have become a very barren place indeed.

In reality, there hasn't been an American movie in the last twenty years as good as *Godfather 1* and *2*. Although there have been outstanding films produced over the last couple of decades, many of them are French or Scandinavian or Argentinean or Spanish. Hollywood still makes great films, just not very often.

However, a more reliable answer may be that few subjects for a movie are more compelling than the Mafia. In terms of sheer glamour, the Italian mobster families are hard to beat. But perhaps I have been over-dismissive of the power of the stage to rival Coppola's *Godfather* opus.

The revival a few years ago of Friedrich Schiller's historical drama *Don Carlos* was as seat-grippingly compelling as the intricacies of the Cosa Nostra.

The bleakest of black comedies, Martin McDonagh's *The Beauty Queen of Leenane*, was more intense and cruelly funny than any film I had seen in years.

And my daughters enjoyed *Phantom of the Opera*, when they were 10.

In general however, perhaps I dread the theatre because productions are so frequently quite terrible, and it's harder than in a cinema to simply stand up and walk out after ten minutes. Or at home, to reach for the remote control.

Don't you find the masterpieces of modern theatre already looking a little flyblown? Can anybody think as highly as we once did of Eugene O'Neill's *Long Day's Journey into Night*, or that Beckett, Ionesco, Miller, Brecht can survive another revival without appearing paunchy and sentimental?

I recognize my own inadequacies here – unable to see Gilbert & Sullivan as anything other than torture, incapable of any amusement at a single sentence by Michael Frayn. But you don't have to be a theatrical romantic to see that we do not have many a Molière or Chekhov or Strindberg writing today.

Did you know that living among us are Marlovians?

They are the adherents to a belief that playwright Christopher Marlowe actually authored the works attributed to Shakespeare; they argue that scholars identify the obvious similarities between Marlowe's and Shakespeare's work; further they point out that though the pair were only born two months apart, the first time Shakespeare is known to have been connected with any literary work was with the publication of *Venus and Adonis*, a fortnight after Marlowe's death – a death which Marlovians believe was faked in a complicated conspiracy theory.

The tale sounds like it would make a popular play in itself, or even a Hollywood film, with Ralph Fiennes as Shakespeare and Orlando Bloom as Marlowe.

Naturally, I would be avoiding both.

Note: The impotence of theatre today is revealed by the fact that a great modern play, the acerbic and morally ambiguous *Becky Shaw* by Gina Gionfriddo, which I gratefully lapped up at the Almeida early last year, couldn't secure a transfer to the West End as producers had filled Shaftesbury Avenue with bits of recycled tosh and flatulent musicals.

Pablo Picasso and Brigitte Bardot in his studio at Vallauris, near Cannes, 1956

YOUR TOUR GUIDE TO ARTIST STUDIOS.

I visited Andy Warhol's studio when his career was at a low ebb. He had achieved great attention in the Pop era, but by the late-Seventies he was considered rather undignified by the art world, because he would paint commissioned portraits of rich people or celebrities.

Nobody much was particularly interested in his work at the time; he was thought to be simply re-working his greatest hits, making multiple versions of his signature paintings in a bulging colour swatch of variants.

From underneath his bed, Warhol pulled out a rolled canvas of *100 Marilyns*, 18ft long, which he had made in 1962. He considered it his masterpiece, and he was saving it for a rainy day. It must have been very rainy the day I visited, because he offered me the picture, for what at the time seemed an insanely high price, but one that I was most grateful to accept as I too believed it to be his greatest work.

It became the centrepiece of the Warhol exhibition that opened my first gallery in Boundary Road, London in 1985.

I found him completely engaging, and learnt that he kept a box next to his working table where he deposited anything that interested him – photos, newspapers clippings, magazine articles, letters, and any ephemera that had captured his limited attention span. At the end of each month, the box was sealed, the date added, a new box started.

There are over 600 boxes that have been archived, contents varying from a mummified foot, Caroline Kennedy's birthday cake, a 17th century book on wrestling, drawings of Hollywood icons, sketches of Jean Harlow's dress, studies of Clark Gable's boots.

He was a committed shopper, and daily added to his ever-growing collection of biscuit tins, native American folk art, taxidermy specimens, exotic jewellery, perfume bottles, autographed pictures of movie stars,

World's Fair souvenirs, cowboy boots, art deco furniture, dental moulds and his trademark collection of white wigs. Warhol believed department stores and thrift shops were just another form of museum.

He provided me with one of the more interesting days in my life.

I went to Julian Schnabel's studio in 1978 when he had just started working in New York and just before he had discovered the joys of broken crockery. He was magnificent in the certainty of his own genius, a complete belief that he was the natural and only worthy successor to Picasso.

I found him so winning and liked his paintings enough to find this not as toe-curling an experience as it sounds. He then went on to produce five years of quite brilliant paintings that the art world largely derided. These works will look like an extraordinary achievement if brought together to hang in a celebratory show. Let's hope some big-time museum in New York doesn't wait for Schnabel to die before it decides the moment is right.

Of course, these days his skills as a movie director have brought him wider acclaim, with much admired films like *Basquiat* and *The Diving Bell and the Butterfly* proving more popular than his crockery paintings in the art world and with the general public. I'll ask him next time we bump into each other whether he would prefer to be the recipient of a clutch of Oscars, or choose instead a MoMA retrospective of his paintings.

The most abiding memory of visiting Lucian Freud's studio were his eyes, with the gimlet gaze of a Hooded Falcon.
But he made for very relaxing company, quick to be amused at the world and his own peccadilloes. He enjoyed the seedy squalor of his rooms in a posh house in the most desirable part of Holland Park, and living up to his persona as an oddball bohemian.

He particularly liked having the subjects of his portraits accommodate his unconventional late-night work timetable, obviously irksome and time-consuming to each of them over a number of weeks, but also a fine way to dominate the procedure, and examine the frailties that made many of his portraits so powerful. A much wittier and endearing man than he apparently appeared to others.

In truth, I find it a little depressing whenever I visit an artist in one of those buildings housing fifty or so artists' studios, knowing that 49 of those artists would rarely get a visitor of much help to their careers.

I have visited studios where artists have openly wept in despair at the struggle of resolving their work. Some artists are extremely touchy about any criticism; others are equally disappointed if you offer no critique, taking your silence as lack of enthusiasm rather than thoughtful consideration. In reality, my uncertainty and dithering usually means I'm finding it hard to produce a fake orgasm. As I don't buy art to ingratiate my-self with artists, or as an entrée into the social whirl of the art scene, at least artists know that I am there to look at the work, with no additional agenda, not even to necessarily buy the art but to simply keep abreast of currents.

These days leading artists like Damien Hirst and Jeff Koons have mammoth studios and are criticised for having the work produced by assistants, like a production line.

Of course, art world commentators criticised the fact that Warhol was hard-nosed about such matters; his studio, where many assistants produced his screenprints for him to simply sign, was known as The Factory. His view was that if the widespread use of assistants was good enough for Rembrandt and Rubens, it was ok for Andrew Warhola.

The artist whose studio I would most have enjoyed visiting would have been Marcel Duchamp. I wonder what my reaction would have been if I had visited him in 1917, and seen his 'Readymades' – the *Bottle Rack* (exactly that, an unmodified spiky construction for drying bottles, that he bought in a local dry goods store), his *Fountain* (a men's porcelain urinal, the original of which was accidentally thrown out by Duchamp's sister who thought it was garbage), and *Bicycle Wheel* (a standard bike wheel sat on top of a white stool).

I don't for a second believe I would have realised I was looking at some of the most revered landmarks in modern art of the 20th century.

Svenska fiskare.

Surströmming consumers

EVEN VEGETARIANS EAT CELLULOSE.

Though we welcome the regulations that require food manufacturers to detail the ingredients of products on their packets, if you are not a chemist a number of the items are a mystery.

Without wittering on like one of those worthy TV documentaries that I immediately switch off, or a friend-of-the-earth style columnist whose sanctimonious opinions I don't want to share, it doesn't take much probing to feel disquieted by what we routinely ingest.

Cellulose is a natural compound that has a whole raft of industrial uses, usually in the form of cotton or wood pulp. Used in the manufacture of cellophane, rayon and cardboard, you can also find it among the listed ingredients in most processed foods.

Cellulose is edible, naturally derived and non-poisonous; it enhances texture, bulk and creaminess; but it is indigestible to humans and contains no nutritional value whatsoever. Imagine eating tree bark.

However, at roughly 30 per cent cheaper than alternatives such as flour and oil, our food authorities are not interested in restricting its usage, or the maximum amount that manufacturers can use in any one product.

And don't think you can avoid it by buying organic products either – after all, cellulose used to be wood and is therefore 'organic' to some extent.

Another little worry I have is with pre-packaged orange juice labelled '100% natural', 'not from concentrate', and 'no added sugar'. How does the stuff stay fresh with no additives or preservatives, I wonder.

It seems that after the juice is extracted, it is collected and sealed in giant holding tanks and all the oxygen in the liquid is removed – which ensures the juice will store without spoiling for up to twelve months. This allows the manufacturer to distribute its product all year round, regardless of season.

There is just one major downside to this de-oxygenation process: it removes all taste of orange from the orange juice.

The solution to this problem is to re-flavour the juice using a 'flavour pack' – a mix of chemicals carefully formulated for the food industry by the same people that make the world's best-selling perfumes.

I won't be the first to mention that all is not flawless at fast food hamburger chains. But perhaps like me, you didn't know that the most modern method to make sure your burger is rendered safe from E.coli or other meat contaminants, is to douse the meat in ammonia gas.

Ammonia is a particularly effective substance used in fertilizers, oven cleaners and toilet sanitizers. A technique invented by the largest producer of burger patties, it was originally developed as a way to use the cheapest parts of the animal, and quickly became the industry standard.

Luckily, our bodies have become so anaesthetized to mass-produced foods that we don't pass out eating this kind of cuisine. Reading about it is nevertheless slightly queasy-making.

Vegetarians always look a little ill at ease if they are in a restaurant and other people are eating steaks so rare that they are a bit bloody. If it's of any comfort to them, the red juice in meat is not blood.

Nearly all blood is removed from meat during slaughter, which is why you don't see blood in raw 'white' meat; only a minute amount of blood remains in the muscle tissue when you buy the meat from the butcher or supermarket.

Red meats like beef are composed of quite a bit of water, and this water mixed with protein ends up comprising most of the red liquid. But frankly, either way is fine with me. I'm a nice self-righteous vegetarian these days.

Many aspects about food remain mystifying.

1. The Japanese eat very little fat and suffer fewer heart attacks than Britons or Americans.

2. The Mexicans eat a lot of fat and suffer fewer heart attacks then Britons and Americans.

3. The Chinese drink very little red wine and suffer fewer heart attacks then Britons and Americans.

4. Italians drink a lot of red wine and suffer fewer heart attacks then Britons and Americans.

5. The Germans drink a lot of beer and eat lots of sausages and fats and suffer fewer heart attacks then Britons and Americans.

Conclusion: Eat and drink what you like. Speaking English is apparently what kills you.

What is the worst meal you have ever eaten? If you've ever tried surströmming that would almost certainly be the one. It's a northern Swedish dish consisting of fermenting herring, and sold in cans which often distort during storage due to the continuing fermentation.

A study in Japan has demonstrated that the smell emitting from a freshly opened can of surströmming is the most putrid odour of food in the world, more overwhelming than the Korean fermented fish dish Hongeohoe.

This explains why in Sweden the dish is usually eaten outdoors.

Apparently, Swedish sailors in the 16th century found that preserving fish in salt was prohibitively expensive, and it would often begin to rot. When they ran into some Finnish islanders they decided to palm off the rotten fish to them.

The Finns bought the fish, and when a year later the Swedish sailors returned to the island, the locals asked if they had more of their delicious fish. The sailors tried it for themselves, liked it, and found it simple and cheap to make plentiful supplies of rotting herring.

It is now a staple, found in bulging cans in supermarkets all over Sweden.

Elephant in the room

CRIPPLED BY CLICHÉ.

How do you stop yourself from using clichéd expressions which have hijacked the language, that everyone limply uses all the time?

The mindless beginning and ending of sentences with 'absolutely'. Or 'basically', 'literally', 'the fact of the matter is', 'at the end of the day', 'I hear what you're saying', 'to tell the honest truth', 'with all due respect', 'no offence', 'at this point in time', 'to be fair', 'no problem', 'when it comes down to it'.

And expressions in general like:

Bear with me

It's been a rollercoaster of emotions

Do you know what I mean?

No pain no gain

Pot? Black?

What goes around comes around

As if

What you see is what you get

It is what it is

In your dreams/You wish/Dream on

No brainer

Elephant in the room

Been there done that

Chick-lit/Aga-saga

Yadda yadda yadda

On the money

Quality time

Fashion victim/Fashionista/Glitterati

Wake up and smell the coffee

Too much information

Grossed/freaked me out

Chill

Loose cannon

Beeyatch

It's not rocket science

Enjoy!

Lighten up

Shabby chic/Heroin chic/Boho chic

Wake-up call

Worst nightmare

No pressure, then

Joined at the hip

What part of no don't you understand?

Comfort zone

Same old same old

End of

Don't go there

Bad hair day

Suits

No way!

What's not to like

Hello?!

A–lister/B-Lister/Z-lister

Don't give up the day job

Bottom line

Veg out

Personal space

Seriously?!

There is no successful cure for cliché abuse I am aware of, and unfortunately clunky dialogue is just as prevalent in movies. Who can forget the exquisite script from *The Notebook*?

'I love you. I am who I am because of you. You are every reason, every hope and every dream I have ever had, and no matter what happens to us in the future, every day we are together is the greatest day of my life. I will always be yours.'

It continues:

'The best love is the kind that weakens the soul, that makes us reach for more, that plants fire in our hearts and brings peace to our minds. And that's what you've given me. That's what I hope to give to you forever.'

And more:

'You can't live your life for other people. You've got to do what's right for you, even if it hurts some people you love. So it's not going to be easy. It's going to be really hard. We're going to have to work at this every day, but I want to do that because I want you. I want all of you, forever, you and me, every day.'

There's more:

'Summer romances begin for all kinds of reasons, but when all is said and done, they have one thing in common. They are shooting stars, spectacular moments of light from the heavens, a fleeting glimpse of eternity and in a flash they are gone. You are the answer to every prayer I've offered, you are a song, a dream, a whisper, and I don't know how I could have lived without you for so long.'

It takes a special gift to write material like this, one I tragically do not possess. But the *The New York Times* critic found the film 'broke through the barrier, and against your better judgement, you root for the pair to beat the odds against them'.

I clearly am not as closely in touch with my feminine side as I assumed.

Things are equally hackneyed in the world of the lyricist. I often wonder if only a songwriter who feels that nobody is actually listening to the words could have composed the following:

Snap – Rhythm Is A Dancer
I'm serious as cancer
When I say rhythm is a dancer

Duran Duran – Is There Something I Should Know
And fiery demons all dance when you walk in that door,
Don't say you're easy on me,
You're about as easy as a nuclear war

Des'ree – Life
I don't want to see a ghost,
It's the sight that I fear most,
Rather have a piece of toast

Paul Anka – You're Having My Baby
The need inside you
I see it showin'
Whoa, the seed inside ya baby,
Do you feel it growin'

Neil Diamond – I Am I Said
"I am" I said
To no one there
And no one heard at all
Not even the chair

Toe-curling though it is to admit it, I always enjoyed this bizarre image from MacArthur Park, originally a No.1 hit for actor Richard Harris and covered in 1979 by Donna Summer. I see it was written by the legendary Jimmy Webb:

Someone left the cake out in the rain.
I don't think I can take it
'Cause it took so long to bake it
And I'll never get that recipe again… Oh no!

But of course the most irksome genre of all is to be found in the world of business.

'I will give 110%, step up to the plate, hit the ground running, deliver pro-active solutions, and blue-sky thinking, 24/7, in a worst-case scenario.'

Lady in a Fur Wrap, 1577–1580, El Greco

PEOPLE DON'T SPIT AT WOMEN WEARING LEATHER.

I saw a young man spit at a middle-aged woman the other day, mumbling something about her wearing a dead animal. People are more violently opposed to fur than leather because it's safer to harass rich women than a motorcycle gang.

However, spending £500 on a pair of shoes or £750 on a handbag is no longer the sole province of the very rich; it is commonplace, perhaps even a bit common to cover bodies and feet in totemic fashion baubles. I once thought it best not to bother putting a stop on a wife's stolen credit cards, on the basis that the thieves couldn't possibly spend money as fast as she did.

But while you're here, I might as well ask you why people in fashion talk about animal hair as 'fur' while referring to human hair as just 'hair'.

Hair and fur are chemically indistinguishable, and both are made up of keratin. The only difference is the pattern of growth: all over if you are a cat, only in certain areas if you are human.

There is a certain kind of narcissist, the deeply self-satisfied kind, who feels any designer plumage would obstruct the view to their own innate gorgeousness. That would be my kind.

I don't like clothes shopping, and trying on outfits in stuffy cubicles in men's shops, looking hideous in the wrap-round mirrors, is something I attempt as seldom as possible. So every few years I go to Selfridges and buy 10 identical black suits, 20 identical white shirts, 10 identical black shoes and never have to spare a thought about what to wear.

A favourite fashion designer is a small American company whose clothing sells in France. On their label instructions, in French and English, the French part of the label translates: Wash with warm water. Use mild soap. Dry flat. Do not use bleach. Do not dry in the dryer. Do not iron. We are sorry our President is an idiot. We did not vote for him.

The trouble with good taste is that absolutely everybody thinks they have it. But don't you sometimes wonder who actually buys all those really horrible clothes and sofas you see in shop windows everywhere?

All rich people seem to gravitate between two preferred decorative styles for their homes.

Route 1

The sleek marble and glass minimalist expanse associated with top-notch hotels, sometimes all black marble and furnishings, sometimes all white, occasionally a daring mix of both, and sometimes even, a riot of beige, appealing to a formative experience of opulence epitomized by a Penthouse or Presidential Suite. It is the style favoured by many successful interior decorators, their efforts lovingly captured in all their coolth by issue after issue of *Architectural Digest*.

Route 2

The Louis Quinze model, also driven by the desire of the newly-rich to appear refined and elegant, so lots of gilt, ormolu, heavy silk drapes, extravagant pelmets, brocaded wallpaper, ornate cabinetwork, Aubusson rugs and rococo a-go-go.

Again, an early influence would have been the experience of a sumptuous five-star hotel suite, simply reeking of all things cultivated and stately. The decorator's brief is to come as close to Versailles as possible: all rather harmless really, and keeping many craftsmen and designers in gainful employment.

Many people are too governed by the need to display the trappings of wealth; although I have little against those who are deeply motivated by the desire for all life's luxuries, most boat owners name their boats, and the most popular name requested is "Obsession".

People often wonder about which is more powerful – money or knowledge. With lots of money in your wallet, you are wise, you are beautiful, and you can sing as well. But if you want to know what God thinks about money, look at the people He gives it to.

Most of us have an idiosyncratic, rather perplexed view about wealth.

People who chase after money, they are avaricious.

If they want to hang on to their money, they are miserly.

If they want to spend it freely, they are wastrels.

If they can't seem to make much money, they are washouts.

If they don't keep trying to make money, they lack ambition.

If they get it without working for it, they are parasites.

If they accumulate it after a lifetime's hard work, then they are fools who never got much out of life.

It is certainly the case that whenever I have seen a man get rich, his next ambition is to get richer.

Voltaire in 1718 by Nicolas de Largillière

THIS IS NO TIME TO MAKE NEW ENEMIES.

On his deathbed, these were Voltaire's last words, as he was asked to foreswear Satan. As for myself, I can be quite accomplished at making new antagonists on a regular basis. Every time you buy an artist's work, you add to the queue of artists and dealers miffed at the snub of your failing to acquire their own work.

Even in my advertising years, our agency wasn't always beloved by its rivals during our mad dash to overcome all opposition to reach top spot.

We paid exceptionally high salaries to our most talented creative people to stop other agencies attempting to poach them.

When we first paid a wage of £100,000 to a copywriter (let's call him Sam Cooper to spare his blushes), it quickly became such a startling piece of gossip spreading around the industry, that a 'Cooper' became a unit of currency e.g. in the coming years people were paid a Cooper and a half, or a couple of Coopers, as salaries spiralled.

At the time I noticed that the subs writing the headlines in *The Sun* newspaper were top-notch at packing a punch in a few words, and were masters of the art of a good British pun. Wanting to hire these *Sun* writers for the agency, we quickly learned their team of headline specialists were the highest paid journalists in the newspaper business, as highly paid as our own golden boys in their Ferraris, and Lamborghinis.

SARKY GETS NARKY AT CARLA MALARKY – *The Sun* headline on the French leader and his wife's affairs.

NO NOBBY BOBBY KEEPS JOBBY – *The Sun* headline, when a policeman who had a sex change was retained by the police force and given a desk job.

SUPER CALEY GO BALLISTIC, CELTIC ARE ATROCIOUS –

The Sun headline after part-timers Inverness Caledonian Thistle dumped Celtic out of the Scottish Cup.

ZIP ME UP BEFORE YOU GO GO – *The Sun* headline following George Michael's arrest in a men's urinal.

STING'S MASSAGE IN A BROTHEL – *The Sun* headline when pop singer Sting got caught coming out of a massage parlour in the Berlin red light district.

I read all of our newspapers each day, not all of them very thoroughly, but enough to enjoy each of their characters. The outstanding ones are fine-tuned to their readers, sensing what interests or repels them, how to ensnare and captivate them. I marvel at their expertise at winkling out proper news, despite the drastically reduced budgets nowadays for investigative long-term story building. I have always considered it best never to complain if a newspaper article is disobliging. If you can't take a good kicking, you shouldn't parade how much luckier you are than other people. But like a prize fool, I once overlooked the invaluable rule of never picking a fight with someone who buys ink by the barrel.

I was in the New York Hamptons mansion of a publishing tycoon, and it was one of those dinner parties where the host guides the conversation so that the table as a whole has to discuss a topic. As the visitor from Britain, I was asked to express my views on the U.S. Press, which amounted to an unrestrained mad-dog attack on the *The New York Times*, its pomposity and vanity, its overweening grandiloquence, its complacency built over years of being a lofty monopoly, easily illustrated by its arrogance in asking readers to "now turn to page B21" or wherever, to continue reading most of their stories.

My fellow guests looked at me curiously, even pityingly. They turned out to be the Editor, News Editor, Features Editor and Arts Editor of *The New York Times*, and it didn't take them long to show me how robust the U.S. Press can be. When the *Sensation* / Giuliani controversy became a leading NY news story, I got given the steel-toe-cap battering I obviously had coming. I am also quite effective at antagonizing friends with the Tourette's level of self-satisfied advice I confer. A colleague, who always finished people's sentences and interrupted them in full-flow, explained that it was just seen as lively enthusiasm by his friends.

No, I said it's merely that when someone is telling you a story, all you can think about is that you can't wait for them to finish so that you can tell your own story that's not only better, but also directly involves you. That's the enthusiasm your friends are referring to.

However, as I'm not an orator of Cicero's abilities, I am quite familiar with other people trying to share their favourite anecdotes, while I am busy attempting to relay mine. I should always remember that the anagram of 'listen' is 'silent'.

Despite an ability to create enemies without even trying, I am nonetheless ready to dispense guidance on dealing with adversaries attempting to destabilise or diminish you.

An acquaintance had someone at his workplace who was always trying to steal the credit for ideas that go down well, toadied up to superiors, attempted to steal the limelight and be the 'special one'. My advice was to do nothing. Remember that the average person thinks he isn't. If you don't interrupt an enemy when he is making a miscalculation, he will make his own undoing.

People say that Pablo Picasso was a wretched man with many enemies, difficult, petulant, short-tempered – and worst of all, with no sense of humour. Even if this were the case, I care very little whether he was adorable, or deplorable; neither do I care whether William Shakespeare, Leonardo da Vinci or Wolfgang Mozart were self-absorbed, arrogant, pompous creeps.

Geniuses are a different breed. The work they bequeath is too momentous for mortals to dwell on the character defects that may occasionally accompany the supremely brilliant. We all have imperfections, but most of us have little meaningful value to our lives, simply content to be content.

The Flower portrait of Shakespeare, a 19th century painting based on the Droeshout engraving from 1623

THERE ARE WORSE WRITERS THAN ME, PUBLISHED EVERY DAY.

Can I recommend the work of Reverend Robert Shields 1918–2007, who lived in Washington, USA?

After his death he left behind a diary of 37.5 million words, chronicling every five minutes of his life for 25 years. He spent four hours a day describing every detail of his actions from cleaning his fingernails, changing a light bulb, recording his body temperature, blood pressure, detailing his bodily functions. He would sleep only for a few hours at a time so he could describe his dreams.

It appears that he suffered from hypergraphia, an overwhelming urge to write, and as you may notice about my own efforts, with little regard to the avoidance of dullness.

I am not alone in having a low regard for the number of books published by writers with even less to offer than me.

In 1969 *Naked Came The Stranger* became a bestseller in America. It was a literary hoax, credited to 'Penelope Ashe', but in fact written by twenty-four prominent journalists. Organised by *Newsday* columnist Mike McGrady, their plan was to demonstrate how low American literary culture had sunk, with the top sales lists dominated by the likes of Harold Robbins and Jacqueline Susann.

Each chapter was written by a different author, creating a deliberately inconsistent, hodge-podge of a narrative, laced with much sexual titillation. Some of the chapters were apparently too well-written and had to be heavily edited to keep to the wretched standard required. For publicity purposes 'Penelope Ashe' was McGrady's sister-in-law, whose photograph was used for the book's author portrait, and who attended meetings with the publishers.

Naked Came The Stranger spent one week high on the *The New York Times* bestsellers list, selling approximately 90,000 copies. The main protagonist in the novel, Gillian Blake, finds her husband is having an affair, and decides to get her revenge by sleeping with a variety of men, from a progressive rabbi, to a mobster crooner.

The book obviously fulfilled the co-authors' expectations a little too well, because they felt guilty about how much money the book was earning, and went public with their hoax. This only served to increase sales even further.

Clearly I would have done much better to concentrate my limited writing efforts in producing a steaming roller-coaster tale of pill-popping and panty-ripping, heaving with clunky dialogue and witless Wags.

My list of favourite books may not suit all tastes, but no library worth its name is complete without the following:

112 Gripes About the French
A handbook produced to help American soldiers liberating France in World War II, to better understand the charming attitude of French citizens.

The Book of Heroic Failures
A book that glorifies spectacularly hopeless ventures.

English As She Is Spoke
A Portuguese-English conversational guide, prepared by non-English-speaking Portuguese with the help of a French-English phrase book.

The Eye of Argon
An infamously poor heroic fantasy, circulated amongst science fiction fans since 1970, as they felt it set the bar to a new low.

Zabibah and the King / The Fortified Castle / Begone Demons
Written by Saddam Hussein these fine works were, unsurprisingly, best sellers in Iraq.

Le Train de Nulle Part
A perplexing, but admired French novel, as it ran to 233 pages, but written without any verbs.

These books may not lift your spirits, but at least you can lift the books. *Bhutan: A Visual Odyssey Across The Last Himalayan Kingdom* measures 7ft x 5ft, and weighs 133 pounds. It features 122 pages of spectacular images, and showcases a variety of digital, photographic and print techniques.

Each book uses a roll of paper larger than a football pitch, and more than a gallon of ink. The portraits of people are life-size or bigger. The books creator, Michael Hawley of M.I.T. challenged the printers and bindery to make the book, and establish that digital images are every bit as good as traditional film photographs. You can see for yourself if you order a copy from Amazon at $30,000.

But if we are discussing poor writers, do you know what Towel Day is?

Even people who haven't read Douglas Adams's *The Hitchhiker's Guide to the Galaxy* might know that Towel Day is a celebration globally every 25th May, as a tribute by his fans to the late author. They all carry a towel with them on that day, to commemorate Adams's words that 'a towel is about the most massively useful thing an interstellar hitchhiker can have'.

I won't bore you with his reasons. Personally, I believe it is because the book is so utterly wet.

I like the Shakespeare Insult Kit, when you combine one word from each of the three columns below, prefaced with "Thou".

Column 1	Column 2	Column 3
artless	base-court	apple-john
bawdy	bat-fowling	baggage
beslubbering	beef-witted	barnacle
bootless	beetle-headed	bladder
churlish	boil-brained	boar-pig
cockered	clapper-clawed	bugbear
clouted	clay-brained	bum-bailey
craven	common-kissing	canker-blossom
currish	crook-pated	clack-dish
dankish	dismal-dreaming	clotpole
dissembling	dizzy-eyed	coxcomb
droning	doghearted	codpiece
errant	dread-bolted	death-token
fawning	earth-vexing	bewberry
fobbing	elf-skinned	flap-dragon
froward	fat-kidneyed	flax-wench
frothy	fen-sucked	flirt-gill
gleeking	flap-mouthed	foot-licker
goatish	fly-bitten	fustilarian
gorbellied	folly-fallen	giglet
impertinent	fool-born	gudgeon
infectious	full-gorged	haggard

Another fine literary technique would be to embrace the delights of Jane Austen and turn yourself into a quick-fire bestseller; an example was reported in the *Guardian* newspaper.

The public's unanticipated desire for the unusual conflation of Regency romance and the Undead sent Seth Grahame-Smith's zombie mash-up *Pride and Prejudice and Zombies* soaring to the top of Amazon's UK "movers and shakers" chart, which monitors the books which are experiencing sudden demand from consumers.

Already sitting at number three in the *New York Times* bestseller lists, the novel – which sees Elizabeth Bennet and her sisters battling a zombie menace that has descended upon the quiet English village of Meryton – looks likely to make a similar killing in the British market.

The novel features Jane Austen's text interspersed with "all-new scenes of bone-crunching zombie mayhem" from Grahame-Smith. So, for example, when Elizabeth is slighted by Mr Darcy at the ball – "she is tolerable, but not handsome enough to tempt me" – the "warrior code" demands she "must avenge her honour ... She meant to follow this proud Mr Darcy outside and open his throat." She's thwarted, however, when a crowd of "unmentionables" pour into the ballroom, and she and her sisters are forced to draw their daggers. "Mr Darcy watched Elizabeth and her sisters work their way outward, beheading zombie after zombie. He knew of only one other woman in all of Great Britain who wielded a dagger with such skill, such grace and deadly accuracy."

I found another interesting literary parody on Wikipedia. *Shamela* was written by Henry Fielding as a shocking revelation of the true events which took place in the life of Pamela Andrews, the main heroine of *Pamela* written by Samuel Richardson. From *Shamela* we learn that, instead of being a kind, humble, and chaste servant-girl, Pamela (whose true name turns out to be Shamela) is in fact a wicked and lascivious creature, scheming to entrap her master, Squire Booby, into marriage.

The novel is a sustained parody of, and direct response to, the stylistic failings and moral hypocrisy that Fielding saw in Richardson's *Pamela*. Reading *Shamela* amounts to re-reading *Pamela* through a deforming magnifying glass; Richardson's text is rewritten in a way that reveals its hidden implications, subverting and desecrating it.

Richardson's epistolary tale of a resolute servant girl, armed only with her 'virtue' to battle against her master's attempts at seduction, had become an overnight literary sensation in 1741. The implicit moral message – that a girl's chastity has eventual value as a commodity – as well as the awkwardness of the notational form in dealing with ongoing events, and the triviality of the detail which the form necessitates, were some of the main targets of Fielding's skewering.

It seems I am not the only fraud passing myself off as a writer.

Wilfrid Michael Voynich who discovered the manuscript in Italy 1912

IF IT CAN'T BE EXPLAINED BY SCIENCE, TRY A SÉANCE.

There are a surprising number of mysteries on Earth, that science has failed to unravel.

There is the Voynich manuscript – a handwritten book thought to have been created in the early 15th century and comprising about 240 vellum pages, most with illustrations. Although many possible authors have been proposed, the actual writer, script, and language remain unknown.

Generally presumed to be some kind of ciphertext, the Voynich manuscript has been studied by many professional and amateur cryptographers, including American and British codebreakers from both World War I and World War II. Yet it has defied all decipherment attempts, becoming a historical cryptology cause célèbre.

In 2009, University of Arizona researchers performed carbon-14 dating on the manuscript's vellum, which they assert (with 95% confidence) was made between 1404 and 1438. In addition, the McCrone Research Institute in Chicago confirmed by testing the ink that the manuscript is an authentic medieval document. It is housed in the Beinecke Rare Book and Manuscript Library of Yale University if you want to have a go at translating it.

Do you believe in ghosts, alien abductions, psychic phenomena, or the like? I don't, but there is sometimes a niggling doubt when you encounter reports of an event that defies logical explanation.

For example, I was mystified by the Overtoun Bridge dog deaths. Overtoun House is a 19th century country estate in West Dunbartonshire, Scotland, located on a hill overlooking the River Clyde. The house became a maternity hospital, and is now a Christian centre. Overtoun Bridge, which stretches across the Overtoun Burn, gained attention because of the large number of dogs that have leapt to their deaths, over the past decades.

It is not known exactly when or why dogs began to leap from the bridge, but studies indicate that these deaths might have begun during the 1950s or 1960s, at the rate of about one dog a month. The long leap from the bridge onto the waterfalls of the Overtoun Estate almost always results in immediate death.

Inexplicably, some dogs have actually survived, recuperated, and then returned to the site to jump again. These dogs are known to the locals of Dumbarton as "second timers." The dogs have mostly jumped from one side of the bridge, during clear weather, and have mostly been breeds with long snouts.

The phenomena received international attention and the Scottish Society for the Prevention of Cruelty to Animals has investigated, but no satisfactory explanation has yet to be found – and dogs keep leaping still.

Recent space images taken by NASA reveal a hitherto unknown submersed bridge in the Palk Strait between India and Sri Lanka. The construction is made of a chain of shoals, 30km long. The bridge's curvature and composition reveal it was man-made. The first signs of human inhabitants in Sri Lanka date back to the primitive age, 1,750,000 years ago, and the bridge's age is almost equivalent.

Just to make the puzzle complete, there is of course a legend, called Ramayana about a bridge being built under the supervision of a dynamic and invincible figure called Rama. Today, Rama's creation is known as Adam's Bridge, and at NASA, they know it isn't simply a myth.

If someone bet you that they could prove aliens from another planet have been on Earth, would you take the bet? I wouldn't, because it's possible they have. How else could anyone explain the Grooved Spheres, that have been discovered by miners digging in South Africa?

Approximately 1 inch in diameter, and etched with three parallel grooves running round the centre, some composed of a solid bluish metal, some hollowed out and filled with an unidentifiable spongy white substance – and all found buried in Precambrian rock dated to 2.8 billion years old.

The Dropa Stones were unearthed in 1938 on an archaeological expedition in the mountains of China. Found inside caves, under layers of dust were hundreds of stone discs, measuring about 9 inches in diameter – each with a circle cut into its centre and etched with a spiral groove composed of minuscule hieroglyphics, that tell the story of how a spacecraft crash-landed into the mountains. For centuries, the survivors have been referred to locally as the Dropa.

The Antikythera Mechanism was recovered in 1900 by sponge-divers from a shipwreck off the coast of Crete. It was a corroded bronze structure composed of many cogs and wheels. Testing of the object indicated it was made in 80 BC, but an x-ray of the machine revealed it to be highly complex, with a sophisticated system of differential gears, not known to exist before the 16th century.

Yes, like you, I believe they are all wonderfully ingenious hoaxes. But I wouldn't want to bet my house, or even my children, on it.

I remember falling for a BBC spoof on April 1 1957, when they broadcast a programme reporting that farmers in the Swiss canton of Ticino were enjoying a bumper spaghetti harvest, showing strands of the pasta growing to great lengths on their spaghetti trees.

On April 1 1998, Burger King launched a marketing campaign for its 'lefthanded Whoppers'. A press release issued stated that nearly 11 million left-handed customers visited the fast food outlets each year, and that Burger King has recognised the difficulties of holding a hamburger in your left hand, when the product has a natural right bias.

I wasn't quite as naive by 1998, and naturally didn't fall for this one, once it was explained it was a whopper.

Arts & Craft fair at Crystal Palace London, 1850s

ART FAIRS ARE NOT FAIR TO ART.

I don't go to the Basel Art Fair anymore, which I used to enjoy greatly. Now I can no longer escape the feeling that the booths in the Basel Art Fair, so full of glossy art, will be full again for the next Fair in their calendar with shiny agricultural implements in the Basel Farmers' Fair, or in the fair after that with medical supplies in the Basel Pharmacists' Fair.

There is something oddly disquieting seeing the reality of the art market in such high relief, the growing hordes of art buyers and art advisers, swarming over fashionable booths, the art seemingly reduced to mere merchandise.

I've always believed that it is important for artists never to be allowed near an art fair, for fear that the disillusionment with being part of a meat market would traumatise them into abandoning their brushes.

Although I now find fair booths a disrespectful way to display art, most artists accept their dealers' view that it's a good way to have your art seen and sold.

If you are as tediously pompous as me, it's easy to get hoity-toity about the aesthetics of art marketing, constantly bemoaning that art is being treated as a commodity. But of course art collectors were spivvy and profiteering even during the Renaissance.

And art is only a commodity if you choose to make it so.

I rather miss the thrill of exploration, the frisson of anticipation I used to enjoy when wandering around the world's art fairs. Then I became creepily fastidious about the context in which art is viewed.

That said, our house is usually full of messy stacks of paintings I'm too lazy to hang, with empty walls and nails poking out when the work goes off to some exhibition somewhere. Any day now we'll get round to hanging some of the piles of pictures sitting on the floor.

I once suspended a Marc Quinn life-size figure hanging upside down in a small, but tall, guest lavatory. It was a dark orangey rubber cast of his body, looking rather like a shed skin, dangling by its feet so that its head was alongside yours as you sat. I don't normally play silly games with art, but the artist was coming over for supper, and I thought he would appreciate my connoisseurship.

There is a moment in every art collector's life when the few bits and pieces they have hanging on their walls have grown to be too many to display. When you buy something that doesn't fit into your home, and has to be stored in an art depot, you're officially an art collector. Whenever I examine the extent of my obsessive/compulsive relationship with art, I feel I am sliding into the world of the Collyer Brothers.

Homer and Langley Collyer were two American siblings who died in the 1940s, and achieved fame of a sort because of their overwhelming and uncontrollable hoarding of books, furniture, musical instruments and many other items, filling every square foot of their house in Harlem.

They were rarely seen, and had left booby traps in corridors and doorways to protect their collection from intruders. They were both found dead in their home, surrounded by 140 tons of collected items amassed over several decades.

Their parents were first cousins, and the sons were exceptionally gifted, with Homer getting his Bachelor degree in Admiralty Law at Columbia University by the time he was 20. Langley played concert-level piano.

Neighbourhood burglars tried to break into the house, because of unfounded rumours of valuables, prompting the booby-trap defence the brothers created. When the police broke in after being alerted to the smell of the brothers' corpses they found baby carriages, rusted bicycles, bowling balls, a collection of glass chandeliers, camera equipment, the folding top of a horse-drawn carriage, dressmaking dummies, 25,000 books, human organs pickled in jars, hundreds of yards of unused silks, tapestries and fabrics, 14 pianos, countless bundles of newspapers, some decades old, filling every room and hallway from floor to ceiling. The salvageable items fetched less than $2,000 at auction. The house was razed as a health hazard.

I am relieved to know that compared to the brothers, I am merely a low-grade amateur. And it's given me more pleasure showing off new work relentlessly for 25 years, rather than hoarding everything away in a secure warehouse, cackling with self-satisfaction as I stroke all my treasures.

Of course rich art collectors are not always entirely delightful, so some of the art world enjoyed hearing about Steve Wynn, proprietor of mammoth Las Vegas hotels and casinos which display his blisteringly expensive masterpieces.

One of these was a beautiful Picasso, *La Rêve*, a portrait from 1932 of his then mistress, Marie-Thérèse Walter.

The picture was due to be sold the next day to another very wealthy collector for $139 million, the highest price ever recorded for a work of art at the time.

But on the evening prior to the sale Wynn was conducting a tour of his collection to a group of celebrities, when in a gesture of animated ebullience he accidentally put his elbow through the canvas, puncturing it with a six inch tear on Marie-Thérèse's forearm.

The sale fell through, the restoration cost $90,000, the painting was now re-valued at a mere $85 million, and Wynn claimed the difference from his insurers.

They baulked, and Wynn sued them in January 2007; the case was settled out of court.

The Picasso had originally been purchased in 1941 for $7,000, also to an American collector.

But Wynn still has many other superb works, including Van Gogh's *Peasant Woman*, J.M.W. Turner's *Giudecca*, Degas' *Dancer Taking Her Bow*, and a Vermeer masterpiece *Young Woman Seated at the Virginals* decorating his Bellagio Casino Resort Hotel in Las Vegas.

I will be at the Frieze Art Fair as usual this year, because it doesn't require more than a 20 minute cab ride to attend. Despite my curmudgeonly distaste for the cheesy bits of the art market, it is always nice to see queues of enthusiastic visitors at the Frieze entrance.

And it won't be so long before we feel a profound sense of loss when Frieze, Basel, and the other fairs that have mushroomed around the globe, become a glamorous memory of a bygone age, replaced by a virtual stroll around dealer stalls in online art fairs.

Note: Belgian artist Paul Van Hoeydonck created the first work of art to
be found on the moon. He met astronaut David Scott, and created a
small statuette to commemorate cosmonauts who had lost their lives
in the quest for space exploration. It was placed on the moon surface by
the crew of Apollo 15 in 1971.

Darryl F. Zanuck, founder of 20th Century Fox in 1935

TOO MANY COCK-UPS TO REMEMBER, BUT ONE I NEVER FORGET.

Somebody thoughtfully asked me how it feels going from an advertising whizz-kid to a past-it pensioner.

But the reality is even worse.

One mistake years ago stopped me being the Hollywood mogul living in glamorous Beverly Hills that I was supposed to be.

In the late 1960s, David Puttnam and I worked together at the CDP ad agency. He left to start off as a photographers' agent and soon was representing many of the world's biggest names. He was obviously getting bored by his easy success, decided that he wanted to get into the movie business, rang to tell me he was very close to Simon & Garfunkel (giant global stars at the time), that they were desperate to feature in a film, but had so far rejected 16 scripts, and would I like to have a go at writing one.

Having checked with him what a script actually was, never having seen one, I wrote something overnight, gave it to David who swooned with delight at its brilliance, showed it to Warner Bros, who were similarly enthused, and offered to send us both to New York, stay at the swanky Pierre, and present the script to S & G.

I pitched the script to small Paul [Simon] who promptly declared it was the first film he had been offered that he really liked, that Art [Garfunkel] would be back in town in a few days, we should hang about, have a nice time, come back and pitch it to him. Art Garfunkel's reaction to my pitch was quite hard to read as he seemed barely alive, zonked out on something or other. When I'd finished, Paul quickly jumped up and announced "he loved it, just loved it".

David never heard from them again.

This little setback didn't deter him for more than a moment, and soon he returned with a great new thought. "I've got this brilliant idea for a movie about gangsters, played by children, and I've even got a great title *Bugsy Malone*. Will you write the script?" he asked. I had to say no to David, explained that I had decided to start an ad agency with my brother and didn't have any time, but did he remember the sweet lad in the office next to mine down the corridor at CDP, Alan Parker? He would make a lovely job of it, I assured him. Alan and David made the movie, it was a big hit, Lord Puttnam went on to win Academy Awards and become one of the big Studio bosses, and Sir Alan went on to make many widely admired films in a glittering career.

Before you ask, I can't remember anything at all about my script, other than it was truly dismal.

But sadly, I can remember too well that I did squander a real shot at Hollywood powerplay and glamour. Hard to believe, but at one time Saatchi & Saatchi was highly regarded in the City, and raised £350 million (a lot of money in those days – one of the largest ever UK rights issues, and to an advertising company with little in the way of assets).

What made it particularly breathtaking was that the money was raised without an acquisition in place, something simply unheard of, and the cash was just there for us to look around for the right deal. There were two contenders: 1) A giant U.S. ad agency purchase that would take us to the top spot in the world league. 2) 20th Century Fox. Both were about the same price, and like fools we went for the ad agency because we thought we know that business rather than the movie business, forgetting of course that in the movie business nobody knows anything.

I still have absolutely no idea what skills are required for moguldom in Hollywood, but if staring at movie screens endlessly during the formative years of your life are an adequate apprenticeship, I am probably over-qualified.

Do you make mental lists of your all-time favourite Hollywood Leading Ladies? You can imagine how distressing it feels to have lost the chance to be part of their world. In no meaningful order whatsoever here are the ones that spring quickest to mind.

Rita Hayworth in *Gilda*

Grace Kelly in *To Catch A Thief*

Audrey Hepburn *Roman Holiday*

Irene Dunne in *The Awful Truth*

Greta Garbo in *Camille*

Bette Davis in *Jezebel*

Marilyn Monroe in *Some Like It Hot*

Elizabeth Taylor in *Cat On A Hot Tin Roof*

Goldie Hawn in *Overboard*

Julianne Moore in *Hannibal*

Anne Baxter in *All About Eve*

Ginger Rogers in *Top Hat*

Jodie Foster in *Silence Of The Lambs*

Anne Bancroft in *The Graduate*

Ellen Barkin in *The Big Easy*

Jennifer Jason Leigh in *Single White Female*

Jane Fonda in *Klute*

Cameron Diaz in *In Her Shoes*

Diane Keaton in *Something's Gotta Give*

Meg Ryan in *Sleepless In Seattle*

Ashley Judd in *Double Jeopardy*

Elaine May in *A New Leaf*

Deborah Kerr in *The Grass Is Greener*

Gena Rowlands in *Gloria*

Alicia Silverstone in *Clueless*

Demi Moore in *Mortal Thoughts*

Hilary Swank in *Million Dollar Baby*

Patricia Neal in *Hud*

Shelley Winters in *Lolita*

Frances McDormand in *Fargo*

Kathy Bates in *Misery*

Geena Davis in *A League Of Their Own*

Louise Fletcher in *One Flew Over The Cuckoo's Nest*

Ann Blyth in *Mildred Pierce*

Lana Turner in *The Postman Always Rings Twice*

Dakota Fanning in *Man On Fire*

Helen Hunt in *As Good As It Gets*

Lauren Bacall in *Written On The Wind*

Lucille Ball in *The Long, Long Trailer*

Kim Basinger in *L.A. Confidential*

Angelica Houston in *Prizzi's Honor*

Sandra Bullock in *The Proposal*

Barbara Streisand in *What's Up Doc?*

Joan Allen in *The Contender*

Angela Lansbury in *The Manchurian Candidate*

Meryl Streep in *Kramer vs Kramer*

Joan Crawford in *Mildred Pierce*

Barbara Stanwyck in *Double Indemnity*

Carole Lombard in *My Man Godfrey*

Claudette Colbert in *It Happened One Night*

Doris Day in *Pillow Talk*

Eva Marie Saint in *North By Northwest*

Jayne Mansfield in *The Girl Can't Help It*

Michelle Pfeiffer in *Scarface*

Jean Simmons in *The Big Country*

Katharine Hepburn in *The African Queen*

Olivia de Havilland in *The Heiress*

Ingrid Bergman in *Notorious*

Angelina Jolie in *The Changeling*

Tippi Hedren in *Marnie*

Toni Collette in *In Her Shoes*

Kim Novak in *Vertigo*

Joan Fontaine in *Rebecca*

Melanie Griffith in *Working Girl*

Janet Leigh in *The Manchurian Candidate*

Uma Thurman in *Kill Bill*

Dianne Wiest in *Parenthood*

Shelley Duvall in *The Shining*

Nicole Kidman in *The Others*

Sissy Spacek in *Coal Miner's Daughter*

Merle Oberon in *Wuthering Heights*

Glenn Close in *Reversal Of Fortune*

Celeste Holm in *Gentleman's Agreement*

Ellen Burstyn in *Alice Doesn't Live Here Anymore*

Cathy Moriarty in *Raging Bull*

Catherine Zeta-Jones in *Intolerable Cruelty*

Charlize Theron in *Monster*

Holly Hunter in *Broadcast News*

Judith Anderson in *Rebecca*

Connie Nielsen in *Gladiator*

Marisa Tomei in *My Cousin Vinny*

Cher in *Mermaids*

Greer Garson in *Mrs. Miniver*

Lee Remick in *Anatomy Of A Murder*

Maureen Stapleton in *Interiors*

Mira Sorvino in *Mighty Aphrodite*

Cloris Leachman in *High Anxiety*

Judy Holliday in *Born Yesterday*

I thought it best not to include a number of talented women who have emerged in recent years, until they have become fully-fledged screen idols.

Apologies if my waning memory has overlooked your personal favourite.

The unadorned truth however is that not all of life's mistakes are as mistaken as they may have once appeared.

If you were to take a set of pliers to my fingernails, I would admit to being deeply relieved not to be some studio big-wig living in vacuous Hollywood; London is a far more intriguing home, and advertising and art have been fascinating enough to be able to enjoy the film business sitting in the dark with my popcorn, not having to deal with the endless supply of grisly people that inhabit movieland.

Note: Darryl F. Zanuck (1902-1979) one of the founders of the Hollywood studio system, was a Protestant of Swiss descent, and got his first movie job as an extra at the age of eight. He was displaced as boss of 20th Century Fox in 1971 after a power struggle with the board, and his son Richard D. Zanuck, whom he had made Head of Production.

Tyche, Greek Goddess of Good Fortune

IS GOOD LUCK OR BAD LUCK PASSED ON GENETICALLY?

Do you know people whom you think of as just downright lucky, and other people who suffer from bad luck to the point of repetitive misfortune disorder?

There is no medical support for my belief in a bad luck or good luck gene; a gene that is simply inherited in the same way as large ears, a prominent chin, obesity, being quick-witted, or being slower but more methodical.

It is simpler to argue that people are born to be both fortuitous and ill-fated in equal measure, and there are some convincing examples.

Vesna Vulović, an air stewardess on a Serbian airline in 1972, would certainly be a benchmark of someone who had both good and bad luck, simultaneously. In January 1972, Ms. Vulović was working an extra shift due to a clerical error. Some terrorists decided to blow up the plane, and did so when it had reached 33,000 ft.

Not only did she survive the explosion that blew the plane to pieces, but she then survived the fall onto the side of a mountain. It was winter and -20c, and though she broke many bones and was found in a coma, when she woke up she asked for a cigarette. Through sheer will, she overcame her paralysis, and regained her ability to walk.

Some would argue she was lucky to have survived falling off the equivalent of 26 Empire State Buildings. Others would say she was unlucky to have been the victim of a clerical error, or she wouldn't have been on the plane at all.

For Vesna, it was just a bad day at the office.

Of course bad luck is often a result of stupidity. In New York in 1977, a man was knocked down by a car, and got up uninjured. But a bystander suggested he feign injury, lay back down in front of the car, in order to collect an insurance claim. The car rolled forward and crushed him to death. Unlucky? Or foolish? Greed can ensure both.

Franz Reichelt, a tailor, fell to his death in 1912 from the first deck of the Eiffel Tower while testing his invention, the overcoat parachute, on its maiden flight.

Poor Tennessee Williams, the author and playwright, died in 1983 when he choked on an eye drop bottle-cap in his room at the Hotel Elysee in New York. He would routinely place the cap in his mouth, lean back and place his eye drops in each eye.

On a personal basis, and more plausibly, I could follow in the path of Marcus Garvey who died in 1940 as a result of reading a negative premature obituary about himself.

Many inexplicable coincidences I would also apportion to a bad luck gene.

Major Summerford was a British officer who retired from the army because of injury. He had been hit by lightning which had immobilised him from the waist down. He moved to Vancouver, where he liked to fish. Unfortunately, the tree he was sitting under whilst fishing was struck by lightning, paralyzing his entire left side. However he managed to recover, and was able to take gentle walks in the local park. But during one of his walks he was hit by lightning that now immobilised his entire body. He died two years later. Four years after that, the cemetery he was buried in was hit by lightning and his tombstone destroyed.

In 1979 the German magazine *Das Besteran* ran a writing competition with readers being asked to send in unusual stories, which had to be based on true incidents. The winner, Walter Kellner of Munich, had his story published. He wrote about the time when he was flying a Cessna 421 between Sardinia and Sicily, and encountered engine trouble. Landing in open sea, he spent some days in an emergency dinghy and was then rescued. This story was spotted by an Austrian, also named Walter Kellner, who said the German Kellner had plagiarized the story. The Austrian Kellner reported that he had flown a Cessna 421 over the same sea, experienced engine trouble and was forced to land in Sardinia. The magazine checked both stories, and both turned out to be true.

I liked hearing about another case of stupidity being the inspiration for bad luck, when a 15-year-old boy was stopped and arrested for drink driving at 12.15am; he blew 529 micrograms per litre of breath, more than three and a half times the legal limit. The teenager was taken to the police station for processing, where his mother was called to collect him. She was subsequently stopped and arrested at 2.14am for driving while drunk, twice over the limit. The mother then rang her partner to come and pick her up. He was stopped and arrested at about 3am, drunk driving at two and a half times the limit.

Their tale reminded me that in 1814, a spectator at the London Beer Flood watched as 323,000 gallons of beer in the Meux & Company brewery burst out of their vats and gushed onto the streets. He helped himself to so much free beer he succumbed to alcohol poisoning.

Is Roy Cleveland Sullivan the luckiest or unluckiest man on earth?

Like Major Summerford whom I mentioned earlier, he seemed to attract more than his share of interest from the heavens.

Sullivan has been struck by lightning on seven different occasions, as a park ranger in Virginia, US, but survived all seven direct strikes, between 1942 and 1977.

He was finally overcome by a broken heart, and perished at his own hand over an unrequited love.

All this blather only proves one fact. There are so many people who have lived on our planet, for so many years, there are going to be inexplicable coincidences occurring occasionally, that you can interpret as good fortune and misfortune as you wish. That of course, does not make my bad luck/good luck gene theory wrong.

Young Winston

DEPRESSION IS MERELY ANGER WITHOUT ENTHUSIASM.

I left school at 16, so never experienced the breeding grounds for clinical depression developed at many universities. Students often find the world of academia difficult to cope with, and suicide rates are tragically high.

You could find some solace in Elizabeth Wurtzel's *Prozac Nation* where she details the mental illness she suffered at Harvard. She explains that her mother made her work hard to achieve success in everything from spelling bees to writing competitions.

'She convinced me this would lead to the Holy Grail: Harvard. A place where I would finally be surrounded by people I had something in common with.'

Yet at Harvard her problems compounded; she had a difficult time coping with campus life, despite a strong intellect, and finally attempted suicide. Aside from the fact that going to a prestigious school can't cure unhappiness, such places can also be arenas that foster mental stress.

Harvard alumna Lena Chen wrote of her university, 'The consensus among my friends was that Harvard drives normal people crazy and drives crazy people to suicide. I wish this were an exaggeration, but it's not.'

Certainly the stigma of not coping makes this worse. Julia Lurie wrote about her time at Yale: 'This culture of silence – the expectation that despite any problem you may have, you must come across as happy, productive and successful – leads students to believe that mental health problems are embarrassing and that admitting them is a display of weakness. As a result, students like these can feel alone, or not good enough for Yale's standards. When combined with the already intense and competitive nature of Yale, the culture of silence creates an awful environment in which to be unhappy.'

However true it may be that the sufferings of the very privileged are trivial when compared to the unspeakable hardships suffered amongst the poor of the world, the emotions are nevertheless still real and their burdens can still be life-threatening.

Depression is clearly without mercy, and grips just as firmly those who apparently have everything, and those who clearly have nothing.

I am more pleased than ever that I gave up school to drive a delivery van, which I rather enjoyed. At the time, driving the van sounded far more appealing than the effort required for a double first at Oxford. Today, I wouldn't mind using Oxford as a genial rest home, whiling away my declining years in the delights of academic pursuit.

Older people also get depressed when they find themselves walking into a room and forgetting why they've gone there. I'm not normally absent minded but apparently this happens to people fairly regularly, and they worry about early warnings of Alzheimer's. Gabriel Radvansky, a professor of psychology at the University of Notre Dame, conducted a simple test to unearth the answer to this commonplace phenomenon.

He explains "Entering or exiting through a doorway serves as an 'event boundary' in the mind, which separates episodes of activity and files them away. Recalling the decision or activity that was made in a different room is difficult because it has been compartmentalized."

Radvansky had subjects perform various memory tasks and then had them either walk through a door into another room, or walk the same distance but stay in the room. They used both simulated environments and real-world situations. In both cases the results showed that passing through doorways diminished subjects' memories.

So don't blame yourself. Blame the door.

I often think about the least terrifying way to top yourself. I wouldn't use pills, in case they leave you alive, but brain-damaged. Too sissy to attempt wrist-slashing or self-lynching. And sitting in a car with a tube from the exhaust pipe, slowly expiring from gasoline fumes, is likely to provide you with a nauseous last few minutes.

I have decided that hurling myself from a very tall skyscraper would achieve the certainty of an instant exit, with no pain, and a particularly exhilarating free-fall fairground-ride demise, as close as I will ever get to fulfilling my fantasy of being able to fly.

It would be considerate to ensure you don't land on a car, or someone strolling below; avoid litter penalties by employing a clean-up team to mop up your mess and bin-bag you appropriately.

I still believe in always trying to be an optimist, and start looking for a silver lining before I see a cloud. But sadly, being an optimist doesn't prevent you from being prematurely disappointed with the future.

Try to be guided by Winston Churchill, who referred to his occasional bouts of depression as his "black dog"; he thought of a pessimist as someone who sees the difficulty in every opportunity, and an optimist as someone who sees the opportunity in every difficulty.

There is no good reason to live your days burning with ambition. Workplace stress can frequently contribute to mental health setbacks; about two thirds of sufferers believe that long hours, unrealistic workloads or bad management at work caused or exacerbated their condition. Many ambitious people endure frustrated, unfulfilled lives, forever seeking something 'better', and are overwhelmed trying to overachieve. They would be much happier being less driven. Life is more pleasant without asking too many questions of yourself, or seeking a higher purpose.

Tenacity and staying resolute are simply being obstinate in a way we approve of.

In reality, the best career advice I can offer anyone is: don't be irreplaceable; if you can't be replaced, you can't be promoted.

Picasso was a genius, not only at making art, but for turning his skills into a long-term commercial enterprise. But he was far from being the first great artist whose skill was matched by business acumen.

I hate to sound like a romantic adolescent, but realistically I believe good artists don't generally see art as a career choice; they simply cannot overcome their desire to make art, and will live on little income for as long as they have to, before they start to sell their work – or give up and get a paying job. Alternatively, another favourite occupation for strangely gifted people, with a limited set of skills, is journalism. I happen to be one of the dwindling group that still love the feel of a newspaper page, a sensuous pleasure the internet cannot provide. My admiration for newspaper writers is undimmed, even the breed who are masters of the hatchet, and given the job of pickling the hapless subjects of their newspapers' disaffection.

William Randolph Hearst, or Citizen Kane as he will forever be remembered, was a newspaper baron who in his earlier days searching for sensational stories, sent a telegram to a leading astronomer: 'Is there life on Mars?' it read, 'Please cable 1000 words.' The astronomer replied 'Nobody knows' repeated 500 times.

An editor once admonished his cub reporter, Mark Twain, never to state as fact anything to which he could not personally attest. Twain complied, offering this account of a gala social event: 'A woman giving the name of Mrs. James Jones, who is reported to be one of the society leaders of the city, is said to have given what purported to be a party yesterday, to a number of alleged ladies. The hostess claims to be the wife of a reputed attorney.'

In the choice of a career as a journalist, writing skills could perhaps be useful, but not as useful as a good sense of rumour.

Of course if you are lazy and with limited business ability the fastest route to success is to marry a very rich woman who is too proud to let her husband work. Every sensible man I know has always fantasized about finding, and securing, a lovely wife who is considerate enough to be exceptionally wealthy.

The only friend who pulled off this wonder ended up with a pleasant enough spouse, profoundly rich, but unfortunately also profoundly insecure and jealous and who didn't trust him an inch. If she didn't find strange hairs on his jacket, she simply accused him of having an affair with a bald woman. His marriage enabled him to spend each day of his pampered life indulging his desire to be swanning around posh golf clubs, but perhaps he ended up paying too high a price for membership.

When it comes to enjoying a fulfilling career, making a valuable contribution, some people think a life well-lived would be that of a doctor daily saving lives.

Though insurmountable for me, if you have the necessary brains and ability, I can't think of a more worthwhile path for anyone to follow.

I heard a tale about a heart surgeon taking his car for a service.

He was exchanging friendly banter with the garage owner, a highly skilled mechanic. "I've been wondering" said the mechanic, "considering what we both do for a living, how much better paid you are than me. I'll show you what I mean," he continued as he worked under the bonnet of a car engine, "I check for faults, fix the valves, change the filters, mend the carburettor, put it all back together so it works as good as new. We basically do the same job don't we? And yet you're paid ten times what I am – how do you explain that?"

The surgeon thought for a moment, and smiling gently, replied "Try it with the engine running…".

The Remorse of Nero, John William Waterhouse, 1878

ANCIENT ROMANS DIDN'T THROW-UP THEIR FOOD IN VOMITORIA.

I always believed the myth that Romans would gorge and then vomit their stomachs empty, and continue to gorge again, making their giant feasts into a commitment lasting several hours using this technique.

Vomitoria were the entranceways through which crowds entered and left a building. Romans didn't have a widespread desire to look like size-zero models, so vomiting would only follow a meal where something was off.

Another Roman myth I accepted until I learnt better was that Emperor Nero fiddled while Rome burned. Violins were not yet invented, and apparently, he could not play the lyre. In fact, upon hearing news of the fire, Nero rushed back to Rome to organize a relief effort, which he paid for from his own funds.

He opened his palaces to provide shelter for the homeless, and arranged food supplies to be delivered in order to prevent starvation amongst the survivors. It appears that he was fated to be remembered for eternity as the callous fiddler, because historians never forgave him for blaming the fire on Christians.

Nero did enjoy having a rather spectacular dining room. The Roman historian Suetonius wrote, 'The chief banqueting room was circular, and revolved perpetually night and day in imitation of the motion of the celestial bodies.'

'It is in these luxurious surroundings that Nero, surrounded by fawning admirers, would have indulged in sexual depravity and held banquets which lasted from noon till midnight.'

'All the dining rooms had ceilings of fretted ivory, the panels of which could slide back and let a rain of flowers, or of perfume from hidden sprinklers, fall on his guests.'

The rotating dining room, with a diameter of more than 50ft was a remarkable feat of Roman engineering with a mechanism of spheres beneath the wooden floor, kept in constant movement by water pressure.

What a pity that Nero is not more fondly remembered for his architectural skills.

More recently, other Italians have been the subjects of disinformation. Benito Mussolini, despite his manifold failings as a human being, is credited with 'making the trains run on time'. The railway makeover had actually been in place before Mussolini and the Fascists came to power. And not surprisingly for Italy, their railways' legendary adherence to timetables was more myth than reality.

It doesn't stop Italy being the most glorious achievement mankind has created. _WOW_

Even though I have seen *Spartacus* and *Gladiator* several times and therefore consider myself an expert on Ancient Rome, I have only just found out about Naumachia. It was a spectacle at the Colosseum in Rome, when they would fill the arena with water and have wooden ships battle it out. Participants numbered in their thousands, and as it was extremely hazardous to participate, slaves were mainly obliged to fill the ships.

The water grew red with blood as the ships slugged it out calling on weaponry such as Greek Fire, an early example of napalm used in primitive flame-throwers, that combusted the instant it contacted oxygen. The happy crowds in the Colosseum were entertained as a few thousand would-be sailors were drowned and burnt alive, until only the last boat was left floating. This saga was news to me, and apparently to Hollywood, who will now have a blockbuster ready to go.

I didn't study Latin at school, or much of anything at all. Any sparse knowledge I picked up came from books or TV. Of course, I would now loved to have been a Latin scholar, with so many evocative and timeless

Latin expressions to enjoy; the Romans certainly had a way with words, as well as building their Empire.

Disce ut semper victurus, vive ut cras moriturus – Learn as if you will live forever, live as if you will die tomorrow.

Philosophum non facit barba – A beard does not make a philosopher.

And my favourite obviously: *Quidquid latine dictum sit, altum videtur* – Everything said in Latin, seems deep.

You'll be glad to know that Italian builders are no better than our home-grown ones, and notoriously slow. The great Gothic cathedral of Milan was started in 1386, and wasn't completed until 1803. Work on St. Peter's Basilica in Rome began in 1506, and wasn't completed until 106 years later.

Every time I think it would have been a more genial and fulfilling life as a Roman Emperor, I try to remember that not all great Romans were blessed with good fortune. In 212 AD, the outstanding Lucius Fabius Cilo, an utterly bald Roman Senator, choked to death on a single hair in a draught of milk.

Of course the historical figure I always felt set the clearest path for himself was Attila The Hun in what would today be called his "mission statement". "Happiness lies in conquering one's enemies, in driving them in front of oneself, in taking their property, in savouring their despair, in outraging their wives and daughters."

What he lacked in modesty (his pet sobriquet was The Scourge of God), he made up for in wisdom; he never attempted to take on Rome or Constantinople, instead accepting payments to leave them alone. He succeeded in devastating or annihilating everything else between the Black Sea and the Mediterranean in his short life, before he died on the wedding night of his 214th marriage. In Hungary, Turkey and Central Asia, he remains greatly revered.

Emperor Yongle, 1360 - 1424

IT TAKES A BRAVE MAN NOT TO BE A HERO IN THE RED ARMY.

This was one of Josef Stalin's interesting observations, after ordering his troops to clear minefields by marching across them, and his airforce pilots to down German aircraft by ramming their own planes into them.

But many heroic figures from history have made difficult personal sacrifices, though none compared to Gang Bing. He was a General under Emperor Yongle, the third leader of the Ming Dynasty that ruled China in the early 15th century. General Gang Bing was favoured by the Emperor and so when Yongle decided to go on a hunting expedition, he placed Gang Bing in charge of the palace. Political intrigue was a constant aspect of life within the Forbidden City and Gang Bing knew his enemies would try to turn the Emperor against him.

Yongle's royal harem of seventy-three concubines was strictly off-limits to all but the Emperor himself. If another man dared have inappropriate relations with the harem, he would pay with his life. When Yongle returned from the hunt, an imperial minister accused Gang Bing of just that.

When the Emperor confronted his General, Gang Bing asked for the Emperor's hunting saddle to be retrieved. When the Emperor was asked to search the saddle, he found a leather bag stowed underneath it; inside that bag were Gang Bing's necrotic, shrivelled genitalia.

It transpired that the night before his Emperor left Beijing, the General had severed his own penis and testicles, bagged them, and hid them upon Yongle's own horse. Yongle was so impressed by his General's sacrifice, he elevated Gang Bing to the rank of Chief Eunuch – which was a politically all-powerful position within the court – gave him numerous gifts and proclaimed him a holy man.

When Gang Bing died he was named Patron Saint of Eunuchs and an ancestral hall, the Eunuchs' Temple, was built in his honour. The hall remained in use up until the communist takeover in 1950, when it was renamed the Beijing Municipal Cemetery for Revolutionaries.

I am ready to open a fan club to Chandragupta Maurya, 340–298 BC.

He was born in Bihar, East India, an orphaned commoner who clawed his way from the slums to forge one of the most expansive Empires in India's history.

Not only did he command nine thousand war elephants, and an army of 36,000 – he had a ferocious bodyguard unit of five hundred Greek and Indian women, considered the most deadly fighters amongst his troops.

In order to destroy the Nanda Empire, Maurya simply grasped his bronze sword in a moment of religious fervour, and singlehandedly stormed the ruling dynasty and put into place the enduring Maurya dynasty.

I am available to play Chandragupta in a Hollywood, or Bollywood biopic of his life, if requested.

But how much wiser to have been Pope Stephen VII, who had the foresight to wait for his opponent to be dead before challenging his authority.

He had the body of his predecessor, Pope Formosus, exhumed in January 897, and the corpse seated on the Papal throne. Stephen proceeded with the trial against Formosus, read out the charges that he had 'usurped the universal Roman See in a spirit of ambition, and had committed perjury'.

He was found guilty on all charges.

So although I admire Pope Stephen's tenacity, and determination to settle old scores, the macabre spectacle turned public opinion in Rome against him. Rumours circulated that Formosus' body had washed up on the banks of the Tiber, and had begun to perform miracles.

A public uprising led to Stephen being deposed and imprisoned. While in prison in 897, he was strangled to death. In December 897 Pope Theodore II convened a hearing that annulled the Cadaver Synod, rehabilitated Formosus, and ordered the remains of his body to be returned to St. Peter's Basilica in pontifical vestments.

Poor Pope Stephen had to wait until Pope Sergius III, a bishop who had taken part in the Cadaver Synod as co-judge, overturned the rulings of Theodore in 904, reaffirming Formosus' conviction, and had a laudatory epitaph inscribed on the tomb of Stephen VII.

This tale not only illustrates the lengths a determined man will go to to seek vengeance, but that a patient individual like Stephen will be able to attain redemption even from the grave.

I found this a useful life-lesson for the children in their formative years, creating a stimulating environment of competitive spitefulness, and treachery, helping them cope with the routine day-to-day business practices lying ahead for them.

I always thought being awarded the title Hero of the Soviet Union sounded rather glamorous, and as they used to hand them out to foreign citizens, I always secretly hoped I would one day be considered worthy.

I am planning a show of contemporary Russian art, in the hope I can be awarded it posthumously, if any of the young artists turn out to be global art superstars one day.

After all, even Ramon Mercader, who moved to Moscow after 20 years in a Mexican prison for assassinating Leon Trotsky, was awarded Hero status by the then head of the KGB.

If you were made a Hero of the Soviet Union twice, by the way, you would have a bronze bust of yourself erected on a pedestal.

The only individuals to have received the title four times were Marshal Georgy Zhukov and Leonid Brezhnev.

Zhukov was reputedly awarded his fourth medal for the arrest of Beria, Stalin's out-of-favour sidekick and secret police chief.

Brezhnev awarded it to himself to celebrate his 60th, 70th, 72nd and 75th birthdays.

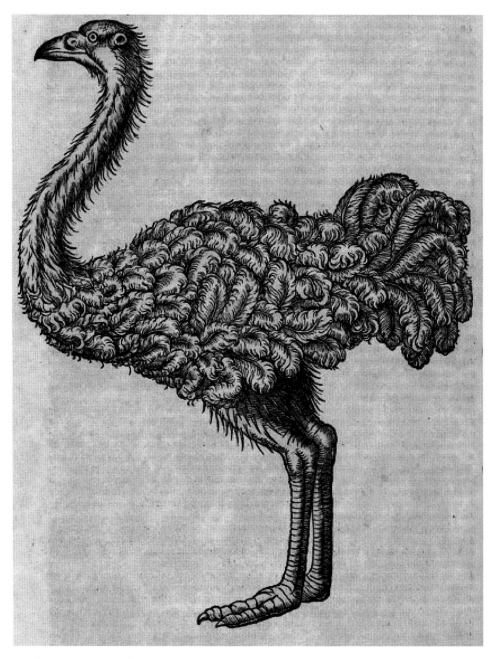

Ostrich by Conrad Gesner, 1516–1565. His studies of animals are considered to be the first modern zoological work

HAVING THE MEMORY OF A GOLDFISH IS PROBABLY BETTER THAN HAVING MINE.

I have been told more than once that I have the brain of a goldfish; supposedly a goldfish has a three-second memory, so they don't go mad in their round glass water bowls, always finding each circle of the bowl is a new experience.

But in reality, this insult was far from being as cutting as it could have been.

Goldfish are a type of carp, and have very good memories for fish. They can be trained to respond in various ways to certain colours of light, different kinds of music, and can remember things they are taught as much as a year later. Researchers have trained goldfish to play fetch, and push levers at the right time of day to obtain food.

Goldfish can recognize their masters, and pick their favourite (usually the ones who feed them.) They have a good sense of time, as they can anticipate being fed if it is done regularly each day.

Because of the fact that goldfish are very intelligent for fish, experts recommend that you regularly change their fish tank around, and make it as intricate and complicated an environment as possible, with much for the goldfish to interact with.

People always claim that humans only use 10% of our brains, but this really isn't the case.

No area of the brain has been found that doesn't have some function, even though that function may yet not be wholly understood. If 90% of the brain wasn't used for anything at all, then damage to that 90% of the brain shouldn't affect a person.

In reality though, deprivation to just about any part of the brain, even tiny amounts of marring, tend to have profound effects.

Probably this myth grew out of a statement by Einstein, suggesting that the human brain has greater capacity for storing information than was thought, and that future generations may be able to improve our access.

Perhaps trials could be conducted on ostriches, whose brains are smaller than their eyes, but are far from stupid creatures. They can outrun a racehorse, and even cheetahs at 70mph have difficulty catching an ostrich because it can change direction very quickly at full speed, and can keep running for a far longer time.

Also, ostriches do not bury their heads in the sand. They quickly lie down if a predator is passing near, so they won't have to expend the energy trying to outrun it.

Does this mean that there is no difference in ability of people with small brains or big brains?

In May 1981 Carl and Elaine Miles, an otherwise unemployed couple, began exhibiting Blackie the Talking Cat on the streets of Augusta, Georgia. Blackie would meow 'I love you' or 'I want my mama' to passersby who would drop coins in the collection box.

After about a month, police warned the couple they required a $50 business license to continue operating. The Miles's purchased a license but sued the city on the grounds that the licensing law was vague, too broad and violated their right to free speech and association. Specifically, they argued that the license ordinance made no mention of talking animals.

The Miles's lost the first round of the case in District Court. They appealed to a Federal Court, and a three-judge panel affirmed the lower court's decision, on the basis that "although Blackie arguably possesses a very unusual ability, he cannot be considered a 'person' and is therefore not projected by the Bill of Rights". Second, they pointed out, "even if Blackie had such a right, they see no need for the applicants to assert his right. Blackie can clearly speak for himself".

Did you hear about the cat with kleptomania?

I hadn't, until somebody suggested I look up Dusty on his Facebook page.

He is a domestic pet who apparently gained notoriety in 2011 as an authentic cat burglar.

He had stolen 16 car wash mitts, 7 sponges, 213 dish towels, 7 wash cloths, 5 towels, 18 shoes, 73 socks, 100 gloves, 1 pair of mittens, 3 aprons, 40 balls, 4 items of underwear, 1 dog collar, 6 rubber toys, 1 blanket, 3 leg warmers, 1 safety mask, 1 pair of pyjama bottoms, 8 bathing suits and a hoard of miscellaneous objects.

Dusty is a Snowshoe cat living in San Mateo, California. His owners began to notice a build-up of household items that did not belong to them appearing in their home.

When his spoils were returned to neighbours by his mortified owners, Dusty became a local personality, and a TV crew set up a motion-triggered night vision camera to catch him in the act of returning with his treasures.

Fans keep his Facebook page updated, providing pictures of the items Dusty brings home each night.

There is so much we don't fully understand about both human and animal behaviour.

Women often ponder what drives so many men to infidelity. Not the obvious ones of proving themselves manly and desirable, but why is their compulsion for promiscuity far stronger than in females?

If we can learn from nature, it's useful to know that during the mating season, male lions mount a female once very fifteen minutes for a solid week, so around 672 different performances. It appears to take a substantial toll, as lions require as much as a two-year hiatus between mating seasons.

Perhaps women could pass on this little lion statistic to their husband / boyfriend / partner, to put him in his place as a masterly seducer.

But please understand it isn't always easy being a red-blooded male.

As Steve Martin said: 'You know "the look" that women get when they want sex? Me neither.'

Gustave Doré, *The Parting of Guinevere and Lancelot*, an illustration from Alfred, Lord Tennyson's *Idylls of the King*

THERE IS NO FUTURE LIVING IN THE PAST.

My teacher at school always drummed into us 'If you want to know the future, look in history books'. But after hearing two eyewitness accounts of the same incident, you begin to worry about history.

Realistically, history is usually lies agreed upon by the victors.

My teacher clearly had a flawless point – mankind is too stupid to have learned from experience, and will continue repeating the same mistakes, over and over again.

People often fantasize about being born into the wrong epoch and would have been happier living in various periods of the past, which they think of as more inspiring than the present.

Nothing wrong in placing yourself in various moments in time, but it is hard to determine what period precisely, contingent on the circumstances on offer. No doubt you would have been happy as a Pharaoh in Biblical Egypt, but not if you had to be a slave, humping rocks up the sides of the pyramid.

Perhaps you can identify yourself as an Emperor in Ancient Rome, but again you may not wish instead to be a candidate for the curtailed life of a gladiator.

You probably feel you would have made an outstanding Knight at King Arthur's Round Table, but may have been a bit nerve-wracked courting Guinevere's favours along with Lancelot, Galahad, Mordred, Gawain, her husband the King, and apparently anyone else who was around while you were all off doing your knightly deeds, and she apparently had nightly deeds of her own.

You might see yourself flowering in the Elizabethan era, a time of gallantry, heroes and adventurers, unless you are press-ganged into the navy, to live your years scourged by seasickness and scurvy. Are you equally sure you would have enjoyed the decades of plague, the lack of general hygiene and proper toilet training?

The Victorian age is simply too Victorian.

I imagine you would have appreciated being revered in the Wild West, as a gunslinger with an immensely quick draw, faster than your pal Wyatt Earp, until a new chap arrives in Tombstone, with an even faster draw – and puts you both in the ground.

It's a 'no' for you to switch to the First World War era, and I also feel that you couldn't possibly have enjoyed the Roaring Twenties with their irritating flappers, gangsters, Prohibition and Charleston.

Perhaps you would have been delighted to have been around in Hollywood's Golden Age, as long as you could dance like Fred Astaire, and look like Gregory Peck.

For myself, it's hard to beat being born in 1943, so that just as you become a teenager, teenagers were invented, along with their own music in about 1956, and nobody cared much about anything, excluding parents who were nervous about total nuclear annihilation, rather needlessly it transpired.

But I am very pleased not to have lived in the 1500s, a period I think would have been hard to take for today's average Londoner.

A little ferreting in the past produces a chilling reminder of the realities of life in the heady days of Henry VIII. Most people got married in June because they took their yearly bath in May, so still smelled comparatively fragrant in June. However, brides carried a bouquet of flowers to sweeten the atmosphere a little. Additionally toothpaste had not been invented and dental hygiene was unknown.

The annual bath consisted of a large tub filled with boiled water, with the man of the house having the privilege of clean water; he was followed by other men in the family and all sons, who were followed by the women and daughters and finally the children, with babies coming last of all. By then the water was so dirty you could actually lose someone in it. Hence the saying, "Don't throw the baby out with the bath water."

The floor was dirt. Only the wealthy had something other than dirt, creating the expression "dirt poor." The wealthy had slate floors that would get slippery in the winter when wet, so they spread thresh (the straw left over after threshing grain) on the floor to help keep their footing. As the winter wore on, they kept adding more and more thresh until when you opened the door it would all start slipping outside. To prevent this, a piece of wood was placed in the entrance way – a "thresh hold."

Bread was divided according to status. Workers got the burnt bottom of the loaf, the family got the middle, and guests got the top, "the upper crust."

Lead cups were used to drink ale or whisky. The combination of lead and alcohol would sometimes render the drinker unconscious for a day of two. They were occasionally taken for possibly being dead, and would be laid out on the kitchen table for a couple of days. The family would gather around for their meals and wait and see if the victim would wake up. The custom became known as holding a "wake."

It was commonplace in those days to dig up coffins and re-use graves. When reopening the buried coffins, some were found to have scratch marks on the inside; they realized they had been burying people alive. So began the fashion to tie a string on the wrist of the corpse, thread it through the coffin and up through the ground and tie it to a bell. A relative would be expected to sit out in the graveyard all night (the "graveyard shift") to listen for the bell. Thus, someone could be "saved by the bell" or was considered "a dead ringer."

So despite the wide variety of unpleasantnesses we are surrounded by in the present day, it would take a brave soul indeed who would wish to venture back to live their lives amongst the Tudors, certainly braver than me.

Edvard Munch, *Self-Portrait*, 1881

MODERN ART CAN MAKE YOU SICK.

I was surprised that someone called Jubal Brown was so inspired by a quiet, even austere abstract painting *Composition in Red, White and Blue* by Piet Mondrian at the Museum of Modern Art, New York, that he vomited onto it.

But he obviously just liked expressing himself in this unusual way, because he later vomited on a painting by Raoul Dufy, *Harbour at Le Havre* in the Art Gallery of Ontario. Mr Brown wasn't charged with vandalism on either occasion, because officials believed his actions had been an accident.

It later transpired that Jubal Brown is a video producer and multi-media artist, and vomited as an artistic performance, presumably in an attempt at gaining celebrity. I am very pleased he has never seen anything at our gallery that he considers worthy of being sick upon.

Of course modern art is more than capable of driving people to seething fury.

I received a very agitated phone call from the Royal Academy on a Friday morning, during the *Sensation* exhibition. Terrible news they said – the Myra Hindley portrait, a 13-foot-high painting based on the child murderer's police mug-shot, created using the handprints of children, had been vandalised.

Apparently, a pair of protestors had hurled paint, ink and eggs at the picture, and the Royal Academy had three leading painting restorers examining it as I arrived.

Restoration expert No.1 gave me the bad news that the 'the ink and egg had fused with the surface of the picture and had become one with the painting' – utterly beyond repair. Restoration expert No. 2 reassured me that given a team of four, and six months working with Q-tips, the picture could be restored by 60-70%, but some shadow residue would persist. Restoration expert No.3 explained about a new technique developed in Japan involving high levels of microwave, that had proved effective on stubborn stains. It was very costly and time-consuming, as each square inch of the canvas had to be microwaved individually.

It fell to me to phone the artist Marcus Harvey, break the news, and ask which of these options he preferred, if any. He asked me to deliver the painting to his studio, and he would see if it was possible to work on it. It was with him by midday.

He rang me early the following Monday morning, and told me the painting was ready to be collected. He had worked on it over the weekend he explained. How does it look, I asked? Perfect he said. Better than before, because it took so long to paint, it had gathered dust while it was damp. Now it looks clean and sharp. What did you do I asked? Lay it on the floor, covered it in Ajax and scrubbed it with a scrubbing brush, he replied.

The picture did indeed look perfect, and was back installed in its room at the Royal Academy that afternoon, but now with its own personal bodyguard.

The point here is that a professional restorer would never, ever, simply scrub a painting with household cleanser. He would have more respect for the artist, and the artwork to contemplate something so foolhardy and callous. Only an artist could treat his own work with such nonchalant brutality.

The *Sensation* exhibition also managed to enrage a number of visitors when it moved on to the U.S.

Someone told NY Mayor Rudy Giuliani there was a painting of a black woman posing as the Holy Mother, and covered by the artist with elephant dung.

What's more, this picture was hanging in his city, in the Brooklyn

Museum, which he funded.

Apparently many ferociously powerful religious groups were enraged, and wanted the painting removed, or the show closed, or the Brooklyn Museum to lose its funding, or even better, all three.

The show became a grenade, presented as a battle between a mad-dog mayor and a groundswell of supporters for the museum from freedom-of-speech activists. The painting's allies wanted to point out that there was nothing wrong with a black artist wanting to paint a black Madonna, and that the elephant dung was merely being used as blocks to support the bottom of the painting off the floor.

The problem for me was that I admire Giuliani, so when the assaults on the museum weren't hitting the right buttons, I didn't enjoy it when his troops switched fire to me, as a pornographer – with previous. 'A history of displaying depraved and sickening works by weirdo so-called artists, for the delectation of superior art snobs'.

The museum was brave, won the day, the rolling news moved on, the show broke attendance records.

Looking back, it seems *Sensation* in London drew its loudest protests about the Myra Hindley portrait.

In New York, it was clearly the Black Madonna. This picture attracted little controversy in London and, though it was clearly not 'covered in elephant dung', it was covered in many detailed close-ups clipped from *Horny Housewives*, which thankfully visitors were quite blasé about.

In Berlin, not a murmur, just happy crowds.

In Australia, show cancelled, when the Australian religious right picked up on the uproar amongst their counterparts in America.

Obviously I'm pleased the exhibition helped establish some of Britain's new artists as household names. And as always, I slither away, the Scheming Svengali wretchedly conjuring all the hoopla in advance, to serve my own perverse ends.

Someone once asked me if I believed art masterpieces are 'stolen to order' for a rich criminal to hoard secretly, or whether that is just a fantasy created in books and films?

I didn't have a clue. But in Paris in 1911, an Italian house painter named Vincenzo Peruggia, angered by incessant French taunts of 'spaghetti-eater' and 'macaroni face', sought his revenge by stealing Leonardo da Vinci's *Mona Lisa*, early on a Monday morning when the Louvre was relatively unguarded.

Surprisingly the theft wasn't noticed until Tuesday at noon. He hid out in a hotel back in Italy where he believed the painting belonged, for more than a year. Peruggia was given a lenient sentence on 'patriotic' grounds by an Italian court. The hotel was renamed Gioconda, after the painting. The Louvre were good sports about it. More visitors visited the museum during this interval – to see the blank space on the wall where the *Mona Lisa* had once hung – than had visited over the previous 12 years to see the painting itself.

In Norway when the Edvard Munch museum lost *The Scream* to thieves for several months, the museum also attracted greatly increased visitor numbers curious to see the empty wall the picture had occupied.

On March 18 1990, two thieves posing as policemen walked into the remarkable Isabella Stewart Gardner Museum in Boston, one of my favourites, and stole thirteen works, including Rembrandt's *A Lady and Gentlemen in Black* 1633, and *Self Portrait* 1634, Vermeer's *The Concert* 1658 – 1660 and Edouard Manet's *Chez Tortoni* 1878 – 1880. There has still been no sign of the paintings, even with a $5 million dollar reward offered by the museum.

It's obviously important for thieves to have a buyer ready for the stolen pieces, as they can be difficult to dispose of through traditional fences. In fact the Munch *Scream* was bought back from the thieves by undercover Norwegian police for only $75,000, though the painting is estimated to be worth well over £100 million.

Art theft at $2.6 billion per annum is clearly a lucrative business for many and currently it is the 4th largest transnational crime after drugs, money laundering and illegal arms trading.

Occasionally, art crime isn't simply about money. Stephane Breitwieser admitted to stealing 238 artworks from museums travelling around Europe; his motive was to build a vast personal collection. In January 2005, Breitwieser was given a 26-month prison sentence. Unfortunately, over 60 paintings, including masterpieces by Bruegel, Watteau, François Boucher, and Corneille de Lyon were chopped up by Breitwieser's mother, Mireille Stengel, in what police believe was an effort to remove incriminating evidence against her son.

Reclining Figure 1969–1970, a major bronze work by British sculptor Henry Moore was stolen from the Moore Foundation on December 15, 2005. Thieves are believed to have lifted the 3.6m long, 2m high by 2m wide, 2.1-tonne statue onto the back of a Mercedes lorry using a crane. Police investigating the theft believe it could have been stolen for scrap value. The Moore is estimated to have been worth £10 million to the right buyer.

Apparently not all art theft is conducted by, or on behalf of, criminal masterminds. In July 1999 a Los Angeles ophthalmologist, Steven Cooperman was convicted of insurance fraud for arranging the theft of two paintings, a Picasso and a Monet, from his home in an attempt to collect $17.5 million in insurance. He was caught when he gamely attempted to cash in once again, trying to sell the supposedly stolen paintings.

MAN BITES MOSQUITO.

An astrophysicist, Lowell Wood, has invented the mosquito laser. It is able to kill large numbers of the insects, reducing the chance for millions being infected with malaria.

The World Health Organization attributes 300 million cases of malaria each year to mosquitoes, and about a million deaths. Reducing mosquito populations also rids the world of the carriers of lethal strains of encephalitis and meningitis, viral diseases that affect the nervous system and the brain, also causing many fatalities.

Dr. Wood was one of the architects of the Strategic Defence Mechanism, known as 'Star Wars', and the mosquito laser incorporates the same technology, scaled down to insects.

As mosquitoes have grown more resistant to pesticides, the laser, referred to by its operators as a WMD (Weapon of Mosquito Destruction) works effectively at wide range, and it is anticipated that when fully coordinated with other scientific technologies developed at NASA, mosquitoes can be largely eradicated in Third World countries at minimal cost.

It may not be as captivating a mission as flying to Mars, but if you have spent a holiday being subjected to even a few itchy mosquito bites, you will be very grateful for this new wave bug zapper.

A different kind of zapper has been invented to reduce the number of rapists.

I was made a little queasy hearing about a new anti-rape condom device – The Rape-aXe sheath. It is a latex condom embedded with shafts of sharp, microscopic barbs that would be worn by a woman in her vagina like a tampon.

If an attacker succeeded in a rape, his penis would be snagged by the barbs, causing him immense pain, allowing his victim to escape. The condom would remain attached to the attacker's body when he withdrew, and could only be removed surgically, which would alert hospital staff and police.

The product was the invention of a South African woman Sonnet Ehlers, who worked as a blood technician and met a number of rape victims. She was inspired to create the Rape-aXe when a patient who had been raped stated, 'If only I had teeth down there'.

Rape-aXe was unveiled in August 2005 in South Africa and although media coverage at the time implied that mass-production would begin in April 2007 the device has never yet been widely marketed and it remains unclear whether it ever will be.

Critics have objected to Ehler's invention as 'vengeful, horrible and disgusting' and opposed its planned sale in drugstores. "It is like we are going back to the days when women were forced to wear chastity belts. Women would have to wear this every minute of their lives on the off-chance that they might be raped." said the Centre for the Study of Violence and Reconciliation, South Africa.

When another critic described it as a medieval instrument Ehlers responded that it was a "medieval device for a medieval deed". Others feared that use of the device could possibly enrage an attacker and further jeopardise the victim. Ehlers replied, "sadly many women have been killed during an attack, as nobody can guarantee the outcome of any rape. However the huge plus-factor is that the pain is such that the rapist would be disabled temporarily giving the victim time to get away and get help".

Pardon me, I'm feeling faint just writing about this product.

Of course they probably have a more technologically enhanced version developed in China.

The world has been a bit slow on the uptake about a number of Chinese advances in recent years, and the command the Chinese have taken across many fields.

Did you know that the world's most powerful computer is to be found at the National University of Defence Technology in Tianjin, named the Tianhe-1A?

It has overtaken the previous record holder, at Oak Ridge National Laboratory in Tennessee, for calculating at breathtaking speeds, apparently reaching 2.5 petaflops, whatever they are.

Supercomputers like the Tianhe-1A can perform a thousand trillion operations per second, enabling them to not only solve the most complex mathematical equations faster than a blink – they can stimulate commercial products like drugs or weapons-related applications.

I always assumed that America's Silicon Valley led the world in this kind of stuff, and was rather floored to discover that the real Silicon Valley is now a fashionable suburb of Beijing.

A thousand years ago China was far ahead of the world in science and technology. They were using paper, gunpowder, movable type printing, the magnetic compass, and had perfected the crossbow, the world's most fearsome weapon.

Explorers like Marco Polo brought back many Chinese inventions to Europe, and the West then took the lead in technology and began to dominate the world, as China entered a more dormant state of development.

Today, once again, China leads the world in many bewildering ways. They are, for example, global leaders in genetic engineering – with the Chinese government directing billions of dollars towards research into modifying genes of crops, animals and even humans.

Dozens of new strains of rice, potatoes, tomatoes, corn and trees have been developed, and there is a program to clone the Giant Panda to save it from extinction.

China also leads the world in mobile banking, spending on luxury goods, high speed trains, the size of its art market, its venture capital growth, in foreign trade, and the export of machinery and electronic products.

It has the world's largest number of broadband subscribers, is world leader in solar energy, and in the use of methanol as an alternative fuel. It also leads the world in the growth of millionaires – and in poverty reduction.

Sadly, China is also very dominant in human rights abuse, is the world leader at executing its citizens, is very stalwart in the use of censorship, and is the biggest jailer on earth of journalists.

Note: The Chinese invented the wheelbarrow with a central wheel enabling it to carry six time as much weight as a European barrow. They were sometimes powered by wind, or beasts of burden, and used an easily maintainable network of narrow paths. Europeans did not adapt to this new technology, and subsequently lost the option of smooth land transportation for almost one thousand years.

Nostradamus (1503–1566) has been credited by his fan club with predicting numerous events in world history, including the attacks on the World Trade Center

NOT ALL CONSPIRACY THEORIES CAN BE CRACKPOT, CAN THEY?

Surely some of them will one day be proven right?

OK, maybe not 'Paul is dead', an urban legend that Paul McCartney died in a car crash in 1966, and was replaced by a look-alike, who could sound-alike. Theorists find 'clues' among the Beatles' many recordings, with some creating symbolic messages when played backwards, and ambiguous imagery on album covers, e.g. Paul is the only barefooted Beatle and is out of step with the others crossing Abbey Road in the eponymous photograph.

I think this tale is as likely as the claim that the Twin Towers had structural failures that were responsible for their collapse, and doctored footage added in the missile-planes. Many witnesses, including firemen, policeman and people who were inside the towers at the time claim to have heard explosions below the aircraft impacts and before they hit their targets, just to confuse speculation even further.

The conspiracy theorists have had a field day with 9/11. Observers with flawless 20/20 hindsight have been quick to point out inadequacies in internal security. They overlook how vigorous America has been at snuffing out the many attacks that were being orchestrated during the last decade.

When faced with trained and determined psychopaths, driven by a demented fervour into large-scale killing, and martyrdom, it is remarkable how effective the West has been at curtailing the intended onslaughts.

On a different dimension of course, there was an earlier occasion when an airplane was flown into a Manhattan skyscraper. On a foggy morning on Saturday July 28th, 1945, a U.S. Army B-25 bomber, on its way to Newark airport, was confronted by dense fog.

The pilot dropped the bomber low to regain visibility, and found himself in the middle of Manhattan, surrounded by skyscrapers. He missed many as he banked left and right, climbing to twist away, but it was too late.

At 9.45am, the ten-ton B-25 smashed into the north side of the Empire State Building on the 79th floor, and the plane's high-octane fuel exploded on impact. One of the engines and the landing gear hurtled across the entire floor, smashing out of the south side to fall onto a 12 storey building across 33rd Street.

The other engine flew into an elevator shaft, and landed on an elevator car, that began to plummet, slowed somewhat by emergency safety devices. Miraculously, when help arrived at the remains of the elevator car in the basement, the two women inside had survived. Many were not as fortunate, and the crash killed 17 people and seriously injured 26 others.

They must have built their skyscrapers very sturdily back then, because the integrity of the building was not compromised, and it was open for business on many floors on the following Monday.

Another skyscraper, 40 Wall Street, known at the time as the Bank of Manhattan Building, was hit by another U.S. Military plane, a C-45 Beechcraft, also headed for Newark on May 20th 1946 at 8.10pm.

It struck the 58th floor, again in dense fog, that reduced the visibility ceiling to 500ft, obscuring the ground for the pilot – but there were astonishingly no reported injuries of any of the 2,000 workers who would have been in the building earlier, nor anyone below on the street. The five crew of the plane were all killed however.

Thankfully today, aircraft are much safer in fog than in the 40s.

Do you believe that God lives inside us all?

God lives on Kolob, a distant star or planet, according to Mormon scripture. In the *Book of Abraham*, published in 1847 by Latter Day Saint prophet Joseph Smith Jr. in a translation from Egyptian Papyri, Kolob is identified as the heavenly body that is the residence of God.

It revolves very slowly, and one Kolob day corresponds to 1,000 Earth years. Unsurprisingly, not all Mormons, and very few non-Mormons share this same confidence about Kolob's landlord, and it appears to be unidentified as either a star or a planet by any astronomical authority.

But one day perhaps, J. Smith Jr. will prove to have been right.

Battlestar Galactica fans may recall the planet Kolob from the TV series, created by Glen Larson, a Mormon.

Were you aware that some people truly believe that Shingō Aomori in Japan is home to the grave of Jesus?

Apparently, the village is convinced that it is the last resting place of Christ, who did not die on the cross at Golgotha.

Instead, his brother Isukuri took his place at the crucifixion, while Jesus fled across Siberia to Mutsu Province in northern Japan, where he became a rice farmer, married and raised a family, near to where is now Shingō.

Local entrepreneurs do a lucrative trade in memorabilia and Jesus souvenirs.

Did you know that up to 20% of Americans, and 28% of Russians believe the moon landings were faked?

They claim that some or all elements of the Apollo program were hoaxes, that the first steps on the moon were simply created on film sets, that faked transmissions, photographs, even rock samples were all a swindle.

Even in Britain, a poll in *Engineering & Technology* magazine found that 25% of those surveyed did not believe that men had landed on the moon.

I am sure that one day, one of the conspiracy theories will be confirmed as fact, and we will all feel foolish when we learn that Elvis Presley and Marilyn Monroe have been based at Roswell, New Mexico during their missing years. Like other aliens from a distant galaxy, they have been living amongst us for centuries, and occasionally take temporary human form, as is the case with JFK, Princess Diana and Paul McCartney.

Bacchus and Ariadne from Marcantonio Raimondi's series of engravings, *I Modi,* 1524

IS IT ONLY PERVERTS THAT DOWNLOAD SEX FILTH ON TO THEIR COMPUTERS?

Some of my primmer friends are blithe about enjoying porn movies, but I have only ever viewed a few particularly sordid scenes; it put me completely off anything to do with sex for some time, possibly as long as an hour.

But do you feel that having pornographic thoughts of a hard-core nature is in itself perversion?

Do you feel that the willing contemplation of vice is vice?

And would you welcome the installation of a robust new branch of the security services, the Thought Police?

Pornography, even the most grotesque kind, has become a pandemic that crosses all age, class and geographical barriers, at all levels of intelligence.

Nobody seems to quite know how to fathom the reality of so much slimy stuff being available on everybody's home screens.

Our new Porn World has taboos of its own, the main taboo being an open understanding of the needs it fulfils, and the consequences. To many people, porn merely represents harmless fun; not to everyone's taste but neither the sole province of strange and seedy men.

China is the world leader in revenues spent on pornography, at over $30 billion. South Korea is only the 26th most populous nation, but with exceptionally high internet use, came in second at $27 billion, followed by Japan and the USA.

The pornography business has larger revenues than Microsoft, Google, Amazon, eBay, Yahoo and Apple combined. 25% of all search engine requests are for pornography, and 80% of 15-17 year olds have had multiple hardcore internet exposure.

America still proudly leads the way in porn production, offering the world over 250 million web pages to browse, and a new porn video produced every 30 minutes.

For all I know, this pornographic ebullience is wholly positive and liberated, clearly meeting the needs of modern society, and doing so effectively with a giddying choice. Even if you, like me, are a bit of a dud at investigating advanced sexual enhancement, wouldn't you like to know more about why we are out of step?

I never did see *Deep Throat*, the first porn movie that entered the mainstream, and was regarded in the public consciousness in a largely positive light.

Deep Throat, reputedly funded with organized crime backing, starred Linda Lovelace and was viewed by 250,000 people in a cinema in Times Square, New York, before censors succeeded in banning the screening in 1973. But by then it was considered chic to view pornography and celebrities at the time including Charlton Heston, Jack Nicholson and Sammy Davis Jr were open in their admiration for the film. Its premise is that Linda cannot achieve orgasm because her clitoris is to be found low in her throat. I won't add a spoiler here, in case you want to see the outcome, but I am told there are many examples of what would be considered hardcore sex scenes, with various methods of penetration, and numerous 'money shots'.

The most famous porn star of the 1970s was an all-American young lady, Marilyn Chambers, who starred in a wildly popular escapade, *Behind the Green Door*, after she was discovered as the wholesome face of Proctor & Gamble's leading detergent brand, Ivory Snow.

Both Linda Lovelace and Marilyn Chambers fared better than the founder of modern pornography Marcantonio Raimondi; during the Renaissance he published a series of engravings in sixteenth century Rome, depicting Greco-Roman figures enjoying the pleasures of copulation. Pope Clement VIII had him imprisoned.

Fanny Hill, first published in 1748 was the first widely read pornographic novel, though banned from public sale in Britain until 1970. Not so long after that, *Playboy* magazine, which had never shown photos of pubic hair or genitals in its early years, would be rivalled by a more graphic newcomer, *Hustler*, with a much more open-door policy. Of course, they have long been overtaken by the swamp of top-shelf material widely available, and a multitude of sex channels on TVs across the globe.

Hurtfully, I have never been asked to star in a porno film, so I find it easy to take a superior air about the whole issue.

But I was asked if it is true that when men die, they get a penis erection. I don't know yet, but if you wish, I will contact you after my passing, and let you know if it is indeed the case, by flushing your lavatory three times at midnight.

I consulted a doctor friend who told me this spectacle was observed only in the corpses of males who were executed by hanging. The phenomenon is attributed, apparently, to pressure on the cerebellum created by the noose. Ladies who were executed were also found to have engorged labia.

Is this why S&M adherents go in for asphyxiation to heighten their sexual peak?

Sorry, I'm simply too squeamish to try it and see.

In general the S&M and Bondage aspects of sex make me go Eek! They sound a bit arduous so I'm not really a suitable candidate for treatment, I'm afraid.

I did once ask room service at the hotel I was living in after a divorce to send out for two large bags of cat litter. My girlfriend who had come round needed them for the cat back at her flat. But the young concierge who delivered them up to the hotel room couldn't hide his blushes, and I can't think what he assumed we might need the cat litter for. His imagination was clearly more colourful than mine, so I must be a bit of a dullard in that dept.

Have you ever written crude words or images on a toilet stall?

I really don't recall, though it is fairly likely as I was a disappointing child in a multitude of ways.

I have enjoyed much lavatory graffiti over the years.

"Please do not throw cigarettes in the urinal, it makes them difficult to light."

"Express lane: Five beers or less."

"Since writing on toilet walls is done neither for critical acclaim, nor financial rewards, it is the purest form of art – Discuss."

"No wonder you always go home alone." [Sign above washroom mirror]

"Members only." [Sign above entrance to gentlemen's lavatory]

Welcome to my world of cultured, urbane humour.

Note: The world centre for the Mormon Church is in Utah, and by coincidence of course, a Harvard study found that the State has the most online porn subscriptions per thousand broadband users in the US.

GVLA.

Pieter Bruegel the Elder, *The Seven Deadly Sins*, detail from *Gluttony*, 1557

SEVEN DEADLY SINS VS. SEVEN HEAVENLY VIRTUES.

Hard to say which of the Seven Deadly Sins I am most guilty of. I rather like all of them, and they are far from being sins; essentially they are all very uplifting and create a balanced and engaged life.

Pride – Without it, what is the point of getting up?

Sloth – Why get up when you can have a nice lie down in front of the TV?

Envy – Healthy in moderation, forgivable in excess.

Lust – Are you joking?

Anger – A meltdown a day keeps the doctor away – fact. I read it in the *Daily Mail*, so it is obviously true that losing your temper regularly is an important health aid to avoid stress and heart attacks.

Greed – Hardly a sin unless it turns you into a sex slave trafficker, drug baron or simply a serial mugger.

Gluttony – Is right up there with Lust.

Strict adherents to the biblical commandments would have to believe that stealing to feed a starving child is wrong.

But if you're looking for a crime here, what about the world's most vile people, who pocket millions given in charitable aid for the hungry, that ends up feeding a few Swiss bank accounts instead?

Or the vast sums that people donate to help refugees or victims of natural disasters, that are mysteriously siphoned off into somebody's private collection of cash?

There are many, many people in need of a bit of retribution, before I would start a vigilante group to hunt down mothers who steal some bread for their hungry children.

It is unforgivable that anybody in the modern world goes hungry or without medical support; politicians everywhere are completely ineffective in doing much about it – or in stemming the widespread corruption that makes a mockery of other people's hardship.

Man's inhumanity to man suggests that our race has not evolved as well as we might have hoped.

In 1963, Yale University psychologist Stanley Milgram set out to test people's propensity to obey authority when ordered to hurt another person.

The world was still trying to come to terms with the horrors of World War II, and Milgram's study made dismal reading. His subjects were told they were to be the 'teachers' of a 'learner'.

They were instructed to deliver electric shocks to the 'learner' (who was secretly complicit in the experiment). They were to deliver electric shocks to the 'learner' if he or she got an answer wrong.

Worse, they were told to increase the shock level if the 'learner' continued to get the answers wrong.

Despite the screams and moans of pain from the unseen 'learner', the subjects continued to deliver even more severe shocks if ordered to do so by the invigilator in the lab coat.

They continued even when told they had rendered the 'learner' unconscious.

It appears we humans are quite easily able to set aside moral and ethical considerations when ordered by authority to violate them.

The artists Pieter Bruegel the Elder and Pieter Bruegel the Younger were both captivated by the wickedness of mankind. But I like the painting called *The Blue Cloak* by Bruegel senior, depicting a land populated by renditions of Flemish proverbs of the day. You can view this painting at the Staatliche Museum in Berlin and happily spend an hour deciphering the proverbs illustrated.

They offer unexpected words of wisdom when translated into English:

Proverb	Meaning
One shears sheep, the other shears pigs	One has all the advantages, the other none
The herring does not fry here	Things do not go according to plan
The scissors hang out there	They are liable to cheat you there
There stand the wooden shoes	To wait in vain
To have toothache behind the ears	To be a malingerer
To bell the cat	To carry out a dangerous or impractical plan
To put your armour on	To be angry
Shear them but do not skin them	Do not press your advantage too far
To be a hen feeler	To count one's chickens before they hatch
Leave at least one egg in the nest	Always have something in reserve
There hangs the knife	To issue a challenge
To have a hole in one's roof	To be unintelligent
To shave the fool without lather	To trick somebody
To play on the pillory	To attract attention to one's shameful acts
To kiss the ring of the door	To be insincere
To see bears dancing	To be starving
To yawn against the oven	To attempt more than one can manage
She puts the blue cloak on her husband	She deceives him
To be a skimming ladle	To be a parasite or sponger
To catch fish without a net	To profit from the work of others

As it happens, I think that the Seven Heavenly Virtues make pretty stagnant fare as a Code of Practice for society.

Chastity – Suggests a stolid and antiseptic life. Worthy, but a trifle colourless.

Temperance – Permanently being sober sounds pretty sombre to me.

Charity – Lovely, and nice work for people seeking knighthoods or a sense of self-regard.

Kindness – Lovely, but malevolent people are more intriguing.

Diligence – Sounds exhausting.

Humility – Why?

Patience – If it's worth waiting for, it's not worth having.

Aldous Huxley, 1894–1963, 'Maybe this world is another planet's hell.'

I AM NOT AS OLD AS I LOOK.

Even if I am too ancient to remember my infanthood, compared to many even older specimens on earth, it seems I am still relatively youthful.

Bristlecone pine trees in the White Mountains of California are over 4000 years old. Many were seedlings when the pyramids were being constructed, but were getting on a bit in the time of Christ.

Creosote bushes in the Mojave Desert are far older however, and one has been identified as being 11,000 years old.

In Tasmania, you will finds King's Holly, a plant with no flowers and no seeds, that is nonetheless surviving at 43,000 years old.

These are mere striplings compared to primordial DNA in bacteria, thriving in ice for 600,000 years, uncovered by researchers in Canada's Yukon Territory.

And the record for the oldest living inhabitants of Earth? It is held by Carlsbad, New Mexico, where spores contained in sea salt have been found to house bacteria in suspended animation, capable of reactivation after 250 million years.

Ask them if they can remember their infanthood, why don't you?

Nature is capable of mystifying us in a multitude of ways.

I remember reading about the Tree of Tenere, a solitary acacia, once considered the most isolated tree on earth, the only one in 250 miles of empty Saharan sand. It was a landmark for caravan routes until it was knocked down by a drunk truck driver in 1973.

In the foothills of the Hochschwab Mountains in Austria is the Green Lake, one of the more unusual natural phenomena on earth.

During the cold winter months, this area is dry, and used as a country park. But as soon as temperatures rise, the snow and ice covering the mountain tops begin to melt, filling the basin and its park with crystal-clear water, with depths extending from 2 metres to over 10 metres.

In June, when water levels are highest, the area is invaded by divers, curious to see what a park looks like underwater. Wooden benches, a grass-covered bottom, trees, roads, even bridges, create a surreal setting for a unique swim in a park.

One of the pleasures of getting old is that you have time to travel the world, and see its wonders. Of course this is not without pitfalls. An elderly friend, though younger than me, was recently in South Korea staying in a three-star hotel, where they insisted the fan in his bedroom was switched off at night, even though it was steaming hot.

Fan death is an urban legend in South Korea, based on the belief that an electric fan left running overnight in a closed room can prove fatal to occupants.

The Korean Consumer Protection Board issued a government-backed safety alert in 2006 warning that 'asphyxiation from electric fans and air conditioners' was among South Korea's most common seasonal summer accidents.

Their warning read 'If fans and air conditioners are left on too long, it causes bodies to lose water and creates hypothermia. If directly in contact with air current from a fan, this could lead to death from an increase of carbon dioxide saturation concentration.'

So there you have it. The hotel was merely concerned for my friend's personal safety, not their electricity bills.

I imagine that as people get older, they begin to fret about the prospects of Heaven or Hell.

I don't think I can imagine anything more excruciating than a Hell where I live at the Hedonism Resort in Jamaica, promenading on the beach in my thong, and then onto their disco – and doomed eternally to do the rounds of Sandals Resorts and Club 18-30 packages.

I was obviously delighted to discover that Hell doesn't actually exist in most respected translations of the Bible.

Hell, in fact, was a creation of Greek mythology and Roman historians. Livy praised the wisdom of an invented fear of a grisly afterlife, 'as a most efficacious means of governing an ignorant and barbarous populace.'

Chrysippus blames Plato for attempting to deter men from wrong with frightful stories of future punishments. Happily, Cicero and Aristotle speak of tales of Hell as 'absurdities and fables'.

Other hereafter destinations that are possibly also fictitious are Heaven, Purgatory, Paradise and Limbo.

It appears there is no logical reason to fear for your long-term future even if you have behaved like an absolute creep your entire existence, I am relieved to report.

But neither can you feel secure that your charitable sacrifices, and kindly deeds throughout your honourable life, will ever receive the perpetual reward you may have anticipated.

Writers and artists have had a field day over the centuries with their versions of Hell. From Hieronymus Bosch and his *Garden of Earthly Delights* or Dante's *Divine Comedy* and Milton's *Paradise Lost*, all have helped create an indelible reminder that bad things happen to bad people.

Like the rest of us, I like Jean-Paul Sartre's 'Hell is other people', but my other favourite students of Hell remain:

Mark Twain
'Go to Heaven for the climate. Hell for the company.'

William Shakespeare
'Hell is empty and all the devils are here.'

H.L. Mencken
'Every man is his own hell.'

Aldous Huxley
'Maybe this world is another planet's hell.'

Of course, many people believe that life is meaningless if you do not believe in God. But the real trouble with atheism is there are no holidays.

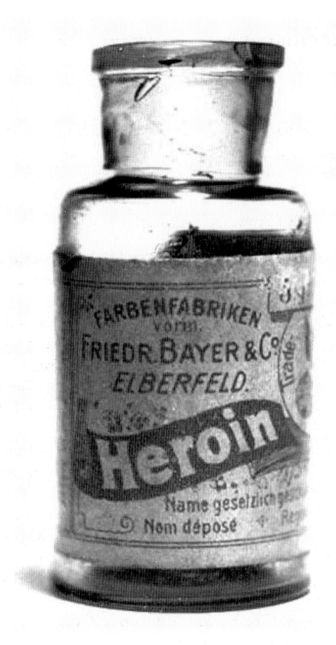

The Boston Medical & Surgical Journal wrote in 1900 about Bayer Heroin's successful launch in America "It's not hypnotic and there's no danger of acquiring a habit".

ARE CHILDREN TODAY MORE ADVANCED THAN WE WERE?

I was a teenager in the fifties, when teenagers were first invented. We had our own new rock 'n' roll music, our imported blue jeans, our black leather outfits, our Elvis Presley greasy bouffants, Marlon Brando's *The Wild One* as our role model – all as a backdrop to our new-found position of significance in the world. We were a horrifying prospect for civilians to come into contact with.

Of course our children today are amongst the international leaders in a number of ways – teenage pregnancies, drug abuse, smoking, drinking, bulimia, anorexia.

My own girls have not succeeded in breaking any world records, and are pretty dull compared to Lina Medina, the youngest confirmed mother in medical history, giving birth at the age of 5 years in Peru.

She was taken to hospital by her parents because of her swelling tummy, and after checking that it wasn't a tumour, doctors determined that she was in the seventh month of her pregnancy.

She needed a caesarean section necessitated by her small pelvis.

Her son was named Gerardo after her doctor. He grew up healthy but died in 1979 at the age of 40 with a bone-marrow disease.

Lina is now 79, lives in Lima, refuses to talk to the countless reporters who have tried to interview her over the years, and has never revealed the father of the child or the circumstances of her impregnation.

If you grew up in the days before Nintendo, Xbox and PlayStation, all you can probably remember as childhood toys were Dinky cars and Scalextric. And possibly Barbie dolls, particularly Ken.

In 1993, Mattel introduced Earring Magic Ken, one of six dolls in the Earring Magic Barbie line. This incarnation of Ken featured an updated look, including blond highlights to Ken's traditionally brown hair, purple shirt, lavender vest, a necklace with a circular charm, and as the name indicates, an earring in his left ear.

Mattel had conducted a survey of girls asking if Ken should be retained as Barbie's boyfriend or whether a new doll should be introduced in that role. Survey results indicated that girls wanted Ken kept but wanted him to look "cooler." The redesigned Ken was the result.

Observers quickly noted the resemblance of Earring Magic Ken to a stereotypical gay man, and with his appeal to kitsch-minded homosexuals, Earring Magic Ken became the best-selling Ken model in Mattel's history.

Despite the commercial success of the doll, public criticism from conservative commentators led Mattel to discontinue Earring Magic Ken and recall the doll from stores.

I wonder what has happened in the lengthy legal dispute between Mattel and MGA Entertainment, who produced the Bratz line of fashion dolls in 2001? In their first five years, 125 million Bratz were sold worldwide, so obviously Barbie was anxious to defend her territory.

Bratz have also endured much criticism about the sexualisation of the dolls' clothing and its effect on children.

Of course these days our children are also better catered for by medical advances since the early days of the last century.

Bayer's Heroin was sold as a non-addictive substitute for morphine, and was a household remedy for children's coughs. Vapor-ol Treatment No.6 for asthma was widely admired for its heady mix of alcohol and opium.

Cocaine Toothache Drops were useful at relieving pain, and keeping children calm and content.

Newborns were also well-catered for with Stickney & Poor's Paregoric, that would ensure untroubled sleep, with its careful blend of opium and alcohol for babies.

Agreed, none of the remedies here can compare with penicillin, or organ transplants, but I think we can agree that they were inventive, and entertaining, nonetheless.

These days people worry that children are no brighter than we were, I fear.

Here are some quotes from eleven year olds' science exams, brought to you via U.C. Berkeley Parents Network.

"Three kinds of blood vessels are arteries, vanes, and caterpillars."

"Vacuum: A large, empty space where the pope lives."

"Dew is formed on leaves when the sun shines down on them and makes them perspire."

"Mushrooms always grow in damp places and so they look like umbrellas."

"The body consists of three parts – the brainium, the borax and the abominable cavity. The brainium contains the brain, the borax contains the heart and lungs, and the abominable cavity contains the bowels, of which there are five – a, e, i, o and u."

"Water is composed of two gins, Oxygin and Hydrogin. Oxygin is pure gin. Hydrogin is gin and water."

I am childish enough to get pleasure from anagrams, probably because I enjoy playing Scrabble so frequently; here are a few of my favourites if you would be kind enough to pass me some of yours:

Desperation > A rope ends it	Mother-in-law > Woman Hitler
Slot Machine > Cash lost in 'em	Woody Allen > A lewd loony
Eleven plus two > Twelve plus one	Princess Diana > Ascend in Paris
The eyes > They see	Princess Diana > End is a car spin
Debit card > Bad credit	A shoplifter > Has to pilfer

This fascination with childish word play has trained me to be a complete bore. It is embarrassing that when somebody asked me why I go to Scott's, the famous fish restaurant, so regularly and eat the same fish dish at every meal there, my answer was a little puerile even for me:

It's not my plaice to carp and rather than flounder or skate around, I cod cast my net wide and say that the sole benefit I am angling for is on the scales.

St Denis of Paris

WHAT'S THE BEST AGE TO BECOME AN ART STAR? 4? OR 94?

Many artists have to wait until they are dead or very old to be appreciated. Not Aelita Andre who in 2011 had her very own solo exhibition at the Agora Gallery in Soho, New York at the age of four. Some of her paintings in the show sold for $27,000.

I hope you find Carmen Herrera, who sold her first painting when she was 89, as inspiring as I do: "Perhaps it's been a good thing I was able to work for so many years without recognition. I was left alone to refine and distil my art for decades, paring things down to their essence. I have no regrets, no complaints, and my work is more important to me than ever. I'm not as well as I would like to be, but as soon as I begin painting all my aches and pains disappear.

"I don't know how I would have reacted if I had been more successful when I was young. Now it's nice, and I have more money than I could ever have imagined earlier in my life. Yet I'm not overwhelmed by it at all. I've always been a private person, and my work is my private life – I'd resent it if I felt people were intruding when I was trying to paint.

"But it is very pleasant to be recognized a little bit – I've made it on to the cover of *The New York Times* without having to kill anyone. All I had to do was get old. The world came to me, eventually. I just had to wait 94 years, that's all."

Picasso consistently pointed out that it took him four years to learn to paint like Raphael and the rest of his life to learn to paint like a child. "All children are artists. Our problem is how to remain an artist when we grow up."

A friend once asked me where would be the best place to sell a large metal sculpture which he had rescued from a skip.

How do you break the news that unless it's by Alberto Giacometti, Henry Moore, Anthony Caro or a few other proper metalworkers, it's best to give it back to the scrap man. You could try a car-boot sale if it will fit in your boot, or if you feel particularly blessed, photograph it and show it to a Sotheby's expert, just in case it's a long-lost Brancusi worth £5 million.

On an encouraging note, in 1820 a Greek peasant on the island of Milos was digging in his field and unearthed several carved blocks of stone. As he burrowed deeper he found four statues – three figures of Hermes and one of Aphrodite, goddess of love. Three weeks later an archaeological expedition arrived by ship, purchased the Aphrodite and took it to France. Louis XVIII gave it the name *Venus De Milo* and presented it to the Louvre, where it became one of the most famous works of art in history.

More recently a couple in a suburb of Milwaukee, Wisconsin, asked an art appraiser to look at a painting in their home. While he was there, he examined another picture that the couple had thought was a reproduction of a work by Van Gogh. It turned out to be an 1886 original. On March 10, 1991 the painting *Still Life With Flowers* sold at auction for $1.4 million.

You probably knew that eBay sells more art than most of New York's galleries put together. I am in thrall to the magnificence of eBay's cornucopia.

eBay sold the original Hollywood sign in 2005 for $450,000.

They found a buyer for the last privately held U.S. Virgin Island. The minimum bid was $3 million and the sale closed on 16th January 2003.

In February 2007, the wife of a DJ sold his Lotus Esprit sports car with a Buy It Now price of 50 pence, after hearing of his flirting with a young model. The car was sold instantly, and the buyer rushed round immediately to collect his purchase.

Water that was reported to have been left in a cup drunk by Elvis Presley was sold for $455.

In 2007, a partially-eaten 10 year old grilled cheese sandwich said to bear the image of the Virgin Mary sold on eBay for $28,000.

In January 2008 four golf balls that had been surgically removed from a carpet python who had inadvertently swallowed them whilst raiding eggs in a chicken enclosure, sold for A$1,700. The python recovered and was released.

Reputedly, the highest price paid on eBay for a single item was the £3.2 million paid for a Gulfstream private jet. But wouldn't you rather have Margaret Thatcher's handbag, sold at a mere £103,000?

Have you ever seen devotional statues in cathedrals of figures carrying their own heads?

When I saw my first one, I was so intrigued I asked the local priest in the Sienese church to help me understand this strange example of early surrealism. His English was very fluent and he explained that they are called Cephalophores.

The saints who are depicted holding their heads in their arms have been martyred by beheading. Displaying the halo in this circumstance added a challenge to the artist, and some placed the halo where the head should be, whereas others have the saint carrying his head intact with its halo.

The most celebrated is Denis, patron saint of Paris, who according to legend miraculously preached in this fashion while journeying from Montmartre to his cemetery.

Poor Nicasius of Rheims was reading Psalm 119 while he was decapitated; after his head fell to the ground, Nicasius' severed head continued delivering the psalm. Saint Gemolo is said to have survived his beheading, collected his head, climbed on horseback to meet up with his uncle the Bishop on a small mountainside, where he gave a final confession.

When the authorities decide to erect a sculpture to me on my passing, my wish is to be depicted holding my head held high, my two arms aloft.

The Wall Street crash, 1929

IT ISN'T BUSINESS. IT'S JUST PERSONAL.

These days, bankers and financiers are reviled as parasites, making too much money and contributing little to society; playing roulette with other people's cash and creating nothing of inherent value – to anyone but themselves.

Whatever the reality, having London as Europe's financial capital, one of the world's top three most influential commercial hubs, is a vital national asset; we haven't been leaders in either light or heavy manufacturing for decades.

But I don't quite understand how 'entrepreneur' is also seen as a term of derision. People once thought of entrepreneurs as buccaneering risk-takers, admired for their business skills at creating a product or service that grew because it captured a market of satisfied repeat consumers.

But I suspect that most people are perfectly able to distinguish between individuals whose success comes from trading financial instruments, and those who have built business empires on inspiration and guts.

Do you remember the early days of FedEx? In 1971, Fred Smith raised nearly $90m from bankers, and put up $4m of his own to build his new company. Unfortunately three years later due to rising fuel costs, the company was on the verge of bankruptcy, with no banks willing to give them any more loans, nor any investors wanting to inject more capital. All the company had was $5,000 to its name, not enough to operate their transport planes.

Smith was desperate, took the last $5,000 to Las Vegas, and played Black Jack over an entire weekend, turning his $5,000 into $32,000, enough to cover the fuel for the planes and operate for a week longer.

He was still driven and determined, and managed to raise another

£11m from a new backer who believed in his vision. It kept the company afloat and by 1976 Federal Express made its first profit of $3.6m.

Today FedEx is valued at over $20bn and Smith himself is worth over $3bn.

Ben Cohen and Jerry Greenfield had the notion of starting a bagel company, but changed their minds when they found out how much it would cost to get all the necessary equipment for bagel baking.

Instead, in 1978 they enrolled on a $5 correspondence course from Penn State University on ice cream making. They managed to pool together $12,000 from loans and savings, and converted an old petrol station in Burlington, Vermont into an ice cream parlour called Ben and Jerry's Homemade.

Jerry had been a lab technician in New York, who had failed three attempts to get into medical school. Ben had attended various colleges, eventually dropping out, and settled on working as a crafts teacher for emotionally disturbed children.

They sold their Ben & Jerry ice-cream business to multinational giant Unilever in 2000 for $326m.

Of course not all entrepreneurs build their business by creating a widely-admired product.

In 2001, global spam was the creation of a somewhat flawed genius, Alan Ralsky, an entrepreneur from Michigan, whose reputation as 'King of Spam' was confirmed when he discovered a way to send millions of emails in bulk promoting a variety of businesses.

When his fame spread, and news of his lavish lifestyle surfaced in newspaper features, many of the recipients of his campaigns wanted to exact the kind of revenge they felt he deserved.

His address quickly swept the internet and thousands of his victims signed him up to every mailing list and free catalogue possible, leaving Ralsky's house with hundreds of lbs of junk-mail dumped at his door each day.

When I say Ralsky was flawed, I should also note that in 2009 he was sentenced to four years in prison for a fraudulent stock manipulation scheme.

People complain that we have perpetually higher taxes, rising prices, worse services. But despite the high cost of living, it remains popular.

And you can be sure of one unfailing rule. When the global economy is in bleak recession, banks are faltering, currencies are unstable, businesses failing, governments teetering, unemployment growing – someone is making a stupendous fortune, that becomes bigger every day.

Many do so by "shorting" e.g. betting on a stock price to drop, or a currency to fall in value, which is what the wiliest hedge fund managers do for sport. The good ones can spot a ship sinking before the passengers on board have noticed a leak. "Short" traders look like magicians, until their bet goes wrong, the ship's leak is miraculously fixed, the passengers sail happily on, and the short traders are left drowning, as the market price moves upwards and against them.

The two clients I most respected when I was in advertising were Procter & Gamble, manufacturers of Pampers, Head & Shoulders, Duracell, Oil of Olay, Max Factor, Tampax, Braun, Gillette, Crest, Fairy Liquid, Ariel, Tide, Mr. Clean, Vicks, Clairol, Pantene, Flash, Ivory, Lenor, Oral B, Bold, Daz, Pringles, Wella, Herbal Essences, etc. etc., making them the most fearsomely efficient consumer goods marketer in the world.

P&G don't want advertising that anyone with creative ambition likes to work on; they rely on a well-tested, fairly straightforward and strictly adhered-to bible for agencies to fashion their ads, and P&G spend freely to make their simple and direct messages lodge in the memories of consumers.

I also had a soft spot for Mars, manufacturers of global brands like Snickers, Bounty, Galaxy, Wrigley, Tunes, Minstrels, Maltesers, Milky Way, M&M's, Twix, Uncle Ben's Rice, Dolmio, and pet foods including Whiskas, Pedigree Chum, Sheba and Pal.

They are the largest privately-owned business in the world, shared wholly between the Mars Brothers, John and Forrest Jnr, and their sister Jacqueline.

Their business headquarters is a low-slung nondescript two-storey building in McLean, Virginia where the Mars Brothers sit in a large open-plan office with well-worn brown wooden desks, amongst the identical ones of the rest of their staff.

They live in two modest suburban houses. John and Forrest Jnr are conservatively worth $15 billion each. When they visited my brother's home in the country, they greatly admired the pretty house set in acres of picturesque rolling hills. My brother suggested that both of them could easily own better houses than this all over the world if they wanted, and with hardly a dent in their bank balances.

They looked most surprised, and reminded him that they both had no actual money, they were merely managers of the business, in preparation for the next generation. Of course when Forrest Jnr wanted a divorce from his long-term wife Virginia, he was somehow able to write a personal cheque for hundreds of millions as settlement.

The Mars Brothers may be different to you and I, but they are much, much brighter and run an organization almost on a par with Procter & Gamble.

If P&G/Mars ever merge, they would make excellent rulers of the planet, and everyone would be very clean and nicely fed, including all pets.

Obviously, I prefer a nice feel-good soap opera about an entrepreneur building a great business through boldness and flair – to hearing that a hedge-fund operator has made billions playing the stock and commodity markets.

Financial manipulators may not be as charismatic and piratical as Gordon Gekko, but they use their computer-like brains to great effect, and they do manufacture something useful, even if it is just money.

But for every success story in commerce there is on overarching theme: for the true entrepreneur, striving for success isn't business. It's just personal.

And remember – you never learn anything by doing it right.

Komar & Melamid's *America's Most Wanted* (top) and *America's Least Wanted* (bottom), People's Choice series, 1994–1997

PAINTING IS A BLIND MAN'S PROFESSION.

"Painting is a blind man's profession. He paints not what he sees, but what he feels, what he tells himself about what he has seen".

This was Picasso's explanation to an observer questioning his methodology.

I can't imagine anything worse than being blind. Somebody asked me if I ever panic that in my world of seeing so much art, my eyesight may fail as I get increasingly elderly. I had never given it a thought until then, and thanked him for placing that at the top of my agenda of disasters to look forward to in my decline.

I recently read about patient TN, who lost his sight after two consecutive strokes had destroyed the visual cortex of his brain. Stroke one had injured just one hemisphere of the cortex, and stroke two did away with the other. He was now clinically blind.

Because, apparently, 'selective bilateral occipital damage' was interesting to researchers where he was recovering in hospital in Geneva, they were keen to examine him, and were amazed to discover that despite his total blindness, he had maintained the ability to detect emotion on a person's face. He responded appropriately – with emotions such as joy, fear, and anger – to a variety of social expressions.

Observed activity in the part of the brain responsible for processing emotions confirmed the curious results. They decided on a further simple yet decisive experiment: an obstacle course. They arranged boxes, chairs and other various objects down a long hallway. The team then asked TN to navigate the course without any form of assistance.

TN was sceptical, as he required the aid of a cane and a guide to get around. But eventually he decided to participate. Researchers recorded the result in their recent paper. 'Astonishingly', the report reads, 'he negotiated the course perfectly and never collided with any obstacle, witnessed by several scientists, who applauded spontaneously when he completed the assignment'.

TN's rare condition is known as Blindsight. Because his strokes damaged only his visual cortex, his eyes remain functional and as a result can still gather information from his environment. He simply lacks the wherewithal to process and interpret it.

Sight has changed for TN from a conscious to a largely subconscious experience. He no longer has a definitive picture of his surroundings, but he has retained an innate awareness, demonstrating to the researchers what they describe as 'the importance of these evolutionary ancient visual paths.'

Is this little tale going to be of much comfort as my eyesight diminishes – to the point where I cannot distinguish between a good painting and a poor one?

It will make absolutely no difference to my judgement, according to a number of my detractors in the art world.

People talk about colours having a noise. I think that 'white noise' apparently sounds like static, and I have heard that it differs from 'pink noise' in ways inexplicable, if you know as little about logarithmic spaces as I do.

I am sure the same applies to 'brown noise', 'blue noise', 'violet noise', 'grey noise', 'red noise', 'green noise', 'black noise'. There is even a 'noisy white' and a 'noisy black'.

They fall under the catch-all reference to synaesthesia.

I promise I tried to follow the answers available in a child's guide to telecommunication electronics, but failed. Synaesthesia in art has been fairly commonplace with artists like Georgia O'Keeffe using titles such as *Music – Pink and Blue*.

In a psychological experiment into synaesthesia first designed by

Wolfgang Köhler, people were asked to decide which of two shapes is named *Booba* and which is named *Kiki*. 95% of people choose *Kiki* for the angular shape and *Booba* for the rounded shape.

Another technical way in which visual interpretation could be measured was by the distinguished Russian artists Komar & Melamid. They decided to conduct a market research survey about aesthetic preferences and taste in painting.

In 1995 they created America's Most Wanted & America's Least Wanted paintings. The survey asked peoples' favourite colour, second favourite colour, preference for outdoor or indoor scenes, religious or non-religious theme, preference for representation of reality or imaginary subject, hard angles or soft curves, vibrant palette or darker shades, preference for geometric or random patterns, wild animals or domestic, older or newer objects for the home, preference for complex images or simple images, preference for children, men or women, figures working, at leisure or posed, one person or a group, nude, partially or fully clothed, historical or celebrated people, ordinary people or famous contemporary people. Etc etc...

The list of questions was exhaustive, and enabled the artists to create the works that the survey decreed would best offer an accurate reflection of what Americans want their paintings to look like, and what they don't want them to look like.

Their interpretations may not be entirely pleasing but as Picasso also said, "the world today doesn't make sense, so why should I paint pictures that do".

I am regularly asked if I prefer abstract art or figurative art.

I try to explain that some people like prawns. Some people like snails. Some enjoy both.

How fortunate am I to like bits of all kinds of art, mincing my way round Italy's cathedrals, France's grand museums, or a student organized pop-up exhibition at an abandoned pie factory.

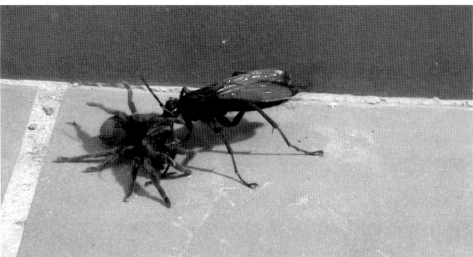

Tarantula Hawk Wasps hunt down tarantula spiders to feed to their larvae

WHAT IS THE MOST PAINFUL MEMORY YOU HAVE?

I had a stomach cramp once as a youth, on the tube at Camden Town. It was piercing, like a violently twisted nerve. I became blisteringly hot, went spookily white, vomiting in agony and terror.

Friends hauled me to the nearest hospital, where doctors could find nothing wrong – the pain had passed as quickly as it had swallowed me, and has never recurred.

I still wince every time I pass Camden Town tube station.

So I enjoyed hearing about the Schmidt Sting Pain Index. It is the work of Justin O. Schmidt, an entomologist at the Hayden Bee Research Centre in Arizona. In 1990 he classified the stings of a number of insects, from 78 species whose venoms he had experienced in his research; each is described in graphic detail, and ranked on a scale with 4 as the most excruciating.

Schmidt Sting Pain Index:

Index	Insect	Description
1.0	Sweat bee	Light, ephemeral, almost fruity. A tiny spark has singed a single hair on your arm.
1.2	Fire ant	Sharp, sudden, mildly alarming. Like a small electric shock you get from a faulty light switch.
1.8	Bullhorn acacia ant	A rare, piercing, elevated sort of pain. Someone has fired a staple into your cheek.
2.0	Bald-faced hornet	Rich, hearty, slightly crunchy. Similar to getting your hand mashed in a revolving door.
2.0	Yellowjacket wasp	Hot and smoky, almost irreverent. Imagine somebody extinguishing a cigar on your tongue.
2.x	Honey bee and European hornet	Like a matchhead that flips off and burns on your skin.
3.0	Red harvester ant	Bold and unrelenting. Somebody is using a drill to excavate your ingrown toenail.
3.0	Paper wasp	Caustic and burning. Distinctly bitter aftertaste. Like spilling a beaker of hydrochloric acid on a paper cut.
4.0	Tarantula hawk wasp	Blinding, fierce, shockingly electric. A running hair drier has been dropped into your bubble bath.
4.0+	Bullet ant	Pure, intense, brilliant pain. Like walking barefoot over flaming charcoal with a 3-inch rusty nail in your heel.

'Nobody likes me, everybody hates me, think I'll go and eat worms. Big fat juicy ones, little slimy skinny ones, oh how they wriggle and squirm etc.'

Did you have this rhyme when you were a child, or did your children use it?

I was a bit disconcerted when my girls started chanting this ditty when they were around seven; they seemed so little to be apparently filled with insecurity and self-loathing.

But as they were giggling happily as they recited the lyric, it became clear this wasn't an angst-filled goth anthem; quite the reverse, a defiantly grisly bit of fun. I got them to stop singing it non-stop, for days, after I told them about the Mongolian Death Worm.

This bright red sausage-shaped creature, 20 inches long and as thick as a man's arm, lives in the most desolate parts of the Gobi Desert. It has no visible eyes, nostrils or mouth, rather like a very lengthy salami, and has the ability to spew out acid on contact, as well as being able to kill humans a foot away with an electric discharge.

Fortunately, it hibernates for most of the year, so you only have to worry if you are in the Gobi in June and July, or a little earlier if the ground is wet, as rain brings the worm to the surface, where they like to attack feet.

There is no known antidote amongst the many aisles in pharmacies stacked with foot medications – corns, verrucas, balms, heel pads, athlete's foot etc. Many people appear to have a lot of trouble with their feet, which thankfully I have managed to avoid. But I do get pretty scared cutting my toe nails, and stab myself attempting to trim them back occasionally – hate long nails.

I once read about detached human feet discovered on the Salish Sea in British Columbia and Washington.

They have discovered twelve of them, seven belonging to men, three to women, two others of unidentified gender, and with two left feet matching two of the right feet.

As of November 2011 only three previous owners of the twelve feet have been identified.

The series of discoveries are particularly baffling as no other body parts have turned up. Teories abound that the feet may belong to victims of a boating accident or a plane crash in the ocean. Foul play has been considered, naturally, but no tool marks for severing were found.

Apparently a human body can survive in water for many years, and a foot may float as far as 1,000 miles.

A *Columbo*-like theory is based on the fact that many of the shoes on the feet were made in 2004, and that the prevailing ocean currents could mean that the feet belong to victims of the Tsunami in that year.

Without being too morbid, I think most of us would prefer fungal infections on our toes, than having our feet wash-up at some sea shore on the other side of the world.

In their selfless efforts to benefit mankind, pharmaceutical corporations have been funding research to develop a pill to erase painful memories.

A study was conducted at the medical faculty of the University of Montreal; volunteers were shown a disturbing video presentation featuring a child whose hand is accidentally mangled when it is trapped in a chainsaw.

Apparently, by taking a pill that reduced the stress hormone cortisol, the disturbing recollections were measurably diminished.

The study was published in the Journal of Clinical Endocrinology, and the hope is that people suffering from post-traumatic stress disorder will find that haunting indelible memories really do become a thing of the past.

Luckily, my memory banks are sufficiently clapped-out not to require medical intervention to alleviate the guilty mementos I have amassed over the decades.

Shizo Kanakuri in 1912

LONDON'S OLYMPICS – BEST ENJOYED ABROAD.

It doesn't matter much to me whether the Olympic Games are held in Singapore or Switzerland. I would be watching them on TV.

But I really didn't look forward to London being desecrated with VIP lanes along our roads for Olympic dignitaries, every street jammed in an August heatwave, my local King's Road Marks & Spencer being engulfed by a billion or two extra tourists.

Instead, you would have found me watching the Games in an air-conditioned bar in some hideaway Italian hotel, along with other temporary expats from London.

Did you ever hear the strange tale about the Summer Olympics in Stockholm in 1912, when Shizo Kanakuri disappeared while running the marathon?

He was listed as a missing person in Sweden for 50 years – until a journalist found him living quietly in southern Japan.

Overcome with heat during the race, he had stopped at a garden party to drink orange juice, stayed for an hour, then took a train to a hotel and sailed home the next day, too ashamed to tell anyone he was leaving.

In 1966 Kanakuri accepted an invitation to return to Stockholm and complete his run. His final time was 54 years, 8 months, 6 days, 8 hours, 32 minutes and 20.3 seconds – surely a record that will last forever.

There was a mildly amusing film, *Cool Runnings*, starring John Candy, a biopic about the Jamaican team that competed in the 1988 Calgary Games. They were not the only Jamaicans who have never seen snow in Jamaica to compete in snow events in Winter Olympics, however.

Lascelles Brown from Jamaica qualified for the bobsled, along with Errol Kerr, in freestyle skiing.

But other countries without a reputation for ski resorts, like Venezuela, Brazil and Puerto Rico, have enjoyed their athletes competing in the luge for example. Competitors in alpine skiing have represented Fiji, Cayman Islands, Senegal, Kenya, Madagascar, Ghana, Costa Rica, Cameroon, Ethiopia.

Perhaps someone should let them know about Monte Kaolino: it's a giant dune consisting of 35 million tonnes of sand, created as a by-product of kaolinite manufacture over the years in Hirschau, Germany.

Now a ski resort, with a ski club for sand ski enthusiasts, it is home to the Sandboarding World Championships.

Its operating season is the reverse of ski resorts elsewhere – it only opens in summer, even though the area does occasionally snow in winter.

I did try a skiing holiday once, and spent a week kitting myself out with a sleek black head-to-toe outfit. I arrived for my first lesson at the appropriate beginner slope at St. Moritz. My instructor was a 12-year-old girl, and I was incapable of taking one step without falling over.

To hide her embarrassment, and my shame, I returned to the hotel, picked up my clothes, left my ski outfit in the hotel cupboard and slunk off to the airport, never to return to ski slopes again.

I also cannot swim, but was told by a friend of mine who was an Olympic swimmer, that because he had to shave his legs, arms and chest for speed-through-water reasons, the hair would always grow back thicker and faster.

However, numerous studies going back to the 1920s show that shaving has absolutely no effect whatsoever on your hair growth rate. Hair growth is controlled by the hair follicles just underneath the skin, and these are not affected in any way by shaving. Only the outer part of your hair is being cut, and that is already dead.

So if you wish to glide through the water as sleekly as you can, feel free.

But after my fortnight in an Italian bar watching our Olympics on their telly, I will return back to London with renewed vigour, once again taking comfort that the best thing about Britain is that it isn't France, and that although London is far from perfection, I adore it.

Our parks make it the loveliest big city in the world, even though every year they are doused in one million gallons of dog urine (a disagreeable thought, but nonetheless true).

There are a number of sports we excel at in Britain, which the Olympic Committee unfathomably refuse to accept into the Games.

The World Toe Wrestling championships started in a pub in Wetton, Derbyshire in the Seventies. The contestants lock their toes together, and attempt to force their opponents' feet to the ground. The organizers applied in 1999 to have it included in the Olympics, but the spoilsports at the IOC declined. Top players include Paul 'Toeminator' Beech, and Alan 'Nasty' Nash, who is the current world champion.

The Annual Worm Charming Championships are not to be overlooked. Held in the lovely village of Willaston, Cheshire, each competitor gets a 3 × 3m plot of ground and has 30 minutes to bring as many worms to the surface as they can. The current world record was established on June 29th, 2009 by Sophie Smith, who raised 567 worms.

What would June be without the World Stinging Nettle Challenge held in Marshwood, Dorset? As you can probably deduce, competitors have to eat as many stinging nettles as possible in an hour. The contest has separate men's and women's sections and both current champions managed to consume 48ft of nettles.

All of these sports would clearly make superb television, but sadly do not make the schedules, nor indeed the Olympic Stadium.

I'm also disappointed that the Zimmer Frame, which I assume I will master any day now, has yet to be accepted as an Olympic competition. And if it were, and were I to win, a further disappointment is that the last time gold medals were made out of real gold was in 1912.

A blue whale's tongue weighs more than an elephant.

INTERESTING FACTS TO BORE A BORE WITH.

If you arm yourself with a factoid gem or two, they can slip into conversational topics whenever required:

Tiger shark embryos fight each other in their mother's womb. The survivor is born.

A blue whale's tongue weighs more than an elephant.

An average person sheds 121 pints of tears in a lifetime.

Duelling is legal in Paraguay as long as both parties are registered blood donors.

Frogs can be frozen solid, then thawed, and continue living.

To "testify" is an expression that grew from the Roman courts, where statements were made by men swearing on their testicles.

Plants develop fevers when they are unwell.

More people die playing golf than any other sport.

Monaco is smaller than New York's Central Park, and Disney World is twice the size of Manhattan.

In the Old West, more cowboys died drowning than in gunfights.

The CIA had an assassination squad called the "Health Alteration Committee".

Donkeys kill more people annually than air crashes.

The microwave was invented when a researcher walked past a radar tube and a chocolate bar melted in his pocket.

The manufacturing documentation to build a 747 airliner weighs more than the airliner.

40% of pizza deliveries arrive faster than an ambulance.

A 'dude' is an infected hair on an elephant's bottom.

Beetles taste like apples, wasps like pine nuts, and worms like fried bacon.

A person will create enough saliva to fill two Olympic size swimming pools in a lifetime.

You could go into more detail about a subject you have boned up on, such as how New York came to be called the Big Apple:

Big Apple was originally horse racing slang to refer to the winnings of a wager. It gradually made its way into the vernacular, with the metaphor that New York City is a succulent and sweet prize to be had by those who are successful in racing, or any field of endeavour.

Have you ever been called a dork, which I certainly was frequently in the 1970s? I thought it meant a slow-witted dullard, but no, it is a simply another expression for penis, a variant on 'dick'.

I can't decide which translation of the insult I feel more comfortable with.

I have obviously been called a 'phoney' more than I'd wish, and checked on its derivation as well, while I was at it.

It evolved from another American slang word, 'fawney', a confidence trick or scam known as the Fawney Rig, where a dud is passed on as a first-class genuine article.

If the conversation is still so dull that you have to draw on this level of inspiration, you could bring up the subject of boat names, or lesbianism, and cleverly interweave the two: *SS Lesbian*, a British cargo ship heading to Malta, was sunk by gunfire from a German submarine during World War I on 5th January 1917.

SS Lesbian, another British cargo ship, seized by Vichy French forces at Beirut during World War II, was scuttled on 14th July 1941. Both ships were named after the inhabitants of Lesbos, Greece, but it has never proven to be an inviting name for a boat.

An even earlier *SS Lesbian* was another cargo ship acquired in 1901, and scrapped in 1903, because its crew all felt a sense of doom and foreboding the moment they set foot on board. Shame really, as it is such a catchy name for a swish yacht.

Included in the Top 10 Most Popular Names List of recent years are: *Fantasea, Sea Ya, Luna Sea, Wet Dream, Liquid Asset, Seas The Day*.

If you are still struggling for conversational time-fillers, you could always ask if your companion has thought about embracing an interest in something unfamiliar, unconsidered by the herd, yet deeply fulfilling to its enthusiasts, something tantalizing enough to captivate you fully?

I have a number of recommendations:

1. Antique Poison Bottle Collectors Association
Sign up at APBCA for their thrice-yearly newsletter.

2. The Belgian Boomerang Association
You might meet the Belgian champion, Corinne Maire.

3. The Cacophony Society
This is definitely you – individuals in pursuit of subversion, pranks and fringe exploration.

4. International Society of Meccanomen
If you throw yourself into Meccano, you could try for the Golden Spanner Award for the most ingenious creation.

5. Israel Vacuum Society
Team up with this group of Israeli academics and learn to be interested in nothing at all – exploring the world of vacuums.

If your companion shows no sign of flagging, and requires even more entertainment from you, there is no choice left – you must simply drop to the floor in a convulsing fit, with spittle drooling from your mouth.

My children have prepared me over the years on how to cope with the stupefyingly dull.

'Finish this: If at first you don't succeed...'

That had been one of my girls' favourites (Skydiving is not for you) when they were small children, falling over themselves at their fine wit.

Another proud moment for my would-be stand-ups was when I was reading them a children's bible story and told them 'The man named Lot was warned to take his wife and flee out of the city, but his wife looked back and was turned into a pillar of salt'.

'What happened to the flea?', one of the girls asked.

They also enjoyed humiliating me with this demonstration of their superior intellect: The pweor of the hmuan mnid.

Aoccdrnig to rscheearch at Cmabrigde Uinervtisy, it deosn't mttaer in waht oredr the ltteers in a wrod are, the olny iprmoatnt tihng is taht the frist and lsat ltteer be in the rghit pclae. The rset can be a taotl mses and you can sitll raed it wouthit porbelm. Tihs is bcuseae the huamn mnid deos not raed ervey lteter by istlef, but the wrod as a wlohe.

My teenage boy likes a riddle.

What runs but never walks, never talks, has a bed but never sleeps, has a mouth but never eats?

What kind of room has no window and no door?

You throw away the outside and cook the inside. Then you eat the outside and throw away the inside. What did you eat?

What gets wetter when it dries?

The more you have of it, the less you see. What is it?

Of course you know the answers, but in case you're as dim as me:

1) River 2) Mushroom 3) An ear of corn 4) Towel 5) Darkness

I get my own back by continuing to recite my favourite truisms:

As a rule, man's a fool. When it's hot he wants it cool. And when it's cool, he wants it hot. Always wanting what it's not.

A rumour is as hard to unspread as butter.

It is easier to be flexible when one is spineless.

An earthquake 4,000 miles away seems less of a catastrophe than the first scratch on your new car.

Any simple problem can be made unsolvable, if enough meetings are held to discuss it.

A penny saved is a penny earned, but a penny spent is a penny enjoyed.

When you see a land of milk and honey, don't count the calories and cholesterol.

But by now, they have already left the room, leaving me babbling away on my own...

It may be true that we are a tiny bit competitive in our family, but I always remind them it doesn't matter whether you win or lose.
What matters is whether or I win or lose.

In truth, the most useful advice I ever gave my children? Never stand between a dog and a tree.

MONS. G. EIFFEL.

From *Revue Illustré.*

Gustave Eiffel, 1832–1923

WHICH IS THE WORST PHOBIA, FEAR OF SPIDERS OR FEAR OF COCKTAIL PARTIES?

I spent many years as a monk in the monastery at Mount Heng, China, perched high on the face of a cliffside, to try and cure my vertigo. People told me that to overcome my fears, it was vital to embrace them.

I'm still working on my terror of spiders. The advice I received was that the next time a spider pops up in your bath, learn to affectionately stroke it before flushing it down the plug hole. There are a number of phobias, which I have happily managed to avoid completely:
1) Botanophobia: Fear of plants, 2) Hypnophobia: Fear of being asleep, 3) Vestiphobia: Fear of clothing, 4) Nephophobia: Fear of clouds, 5) Hedonophobia: Fear of feeling pleasure.

And the most tricky of all phobias to tackle: Phobophobia: Fear of acquiring a phobia.

There is a palpable difference between normal fears and phobias:

Fear	Normal Response	Phobic Response
Flying	Seat-gripping anxiety when the plane hits turbulence; panic during take-off/landing amid bad weather conditions.	Refusing to board the flight even though it means missing your best friend's wedding.
Heights	Butterflies in the stomach at the top of a skyscraper or up a tall ladder.	Turning down a great job offer because it comes with an office on the tenth floor.
Dogs	Jitters when you see a Pit-bull approaching or a Rottweiler growling at you.	Avoiding the local park because there is likely to be a dog or two in there.
Needles	Feeling dizzy at the prospect of an injection or having blood taken.	Going without hospital treatment or missing a GP check-up because of your terror of hypodermics.

Gustave Eiffel, who was clearly more manly and stoic than me, managed to have a successful career as an architect of tall constructions, despite having a paralyzing fear of heights. I found myself getting nauseous just halfway up his Tower, overcome with vertigo to a humiliating level.

The most common phobia, of which I would like to be patron saint, is social phobia, also known as social anxiety disorder – a fear of social situations where you may be embarrassed or judged. With social phobia, you may be excessively self-conscious and afraid of humiliating yourself in front of others.

I find it miraculous to have met so many people without this condition, which I once assumed I shared with everybody.

As I can't swim, one of the few phobias I don't possess is fear of sharks. If you do, and if it's of any comfort, I can tell you that cows kill many more people than sharks each year, fatally trampling 100 people every 12 months. Deer kill more people each year than spiders, snakes, bears and wolves combined. Deer are very effective at parking themselves in front of oncoming cars in dark country lanes.

In any event, the sea is full of other terrifying creatures – jellyfish, sea snakes, eels, barracuda, all kinds of fish with teeth, or poison, or spikes. Stick to the local swimming baths, I think.

There is almost nothing that exists in the world that does not have a phobia available. Here are some of the 'A's':

Ablutophobia – Fear of washing	Aurophobia – Fear of gold
Acerophobia – Fear of sourness	Auroraphobia – Fear of Northern lights
Alektorophobia – Fear of chickens	Autophobia – Fear of being alone
Alliumphobia – Fear of garlic	Allodoxaphobia – Fear of opinions
Ambulophobia – Fear of walking	Amathophobia – Fear of dust
Anablephobia – Fear of looking up	Ancraophobia – Fear of wind
Anthrophobia – Fear of flowers	Arithmophobia – Fear of numbers
Apeirophobia – Fear of infinity	Atephobia – Fear of ruins
Aulophobia – Fear of flutes	Athazagoraphobia – Fear of being forgotten

There is even a common phobia with a double 'A' – Abstract Art. Many people with this phobia firmly believe that nobody would notice if the Rothko paintings at the Tate were hung upside down. But art isn't an IQ test. If an abstract painting looks as bad to you upside down as it would the right way up, it's apparent that neither view would give you much pleasure.

I try to encourage people with this phobia to spare a little time to look into the era when Impressionism grew into early abstraction, and then onto the full-blown freedom that Pollock allowed himself, and see if this small introduction helps them to enjoy many of the key works of the 20th century.

One of the more useless pieces of wisdom handed down is the Franklin D. Roosevelt statement 'The only thing we have to fear, is fear itself'. Even if that were true, it doesn't mean that the sight of a common garden spider doesn't have me squealing like a girl.

Another of my other little fears is of paper cuts. I had no idea why they hurt so much, but got a quick and informed response by checking on the appropriate medical website. Fingertips and hands have more nociceptors (nerve fibres to you) per square millimetre than the rest of your body. Paper hurts more than other cuts to the hand because the edges of paper are dull and flexible, compared to say, knives. A paper cut mutilates the skin more, and though the damage is very shallow, it further increases the pain because the most sensitive nerves in your skin are nearest the surface.

Furthermore, the paper cut will not bleed much, or at all, leaving the nerves open to the air and other irritants, so it will continue to be in an activated state for longer than more significant cuts. Sometimes the paper itself is coated with chemicals, such as bleach, which stimulates the pain further. I also have a phobia about being punctual. But the trouble with being punctual is that nobody's there to appreciate it.

I am always on time, but fear that this is a clear indication that I lead an empty life, with nothing to do but be the first to arrive at dinner parties and restaurants. If you are always prompt, you never experience the grateful anticipation that greets the fashionably tardy.

The official White House portrait of Calvin Coolidge, 1932

KNOWING YOURSELF WELL,
WOULD YOU CHOOSE YOU AS A FRIEND?

What do you like most about yourself? What's the best part of being you? What specific character trait do you want to be known for?

These are some of the unappetizing questions I put to myself in seeking an answer to this; the only comfort I could find was my feeling that those who look for friends without faults will have none.

I did receive a Friendship Card once, but I always feared the greeting message inside was meant ironically.

Some days are cold and dark,
Some make us feel so alone,
Some days are hard to understand,
On those days God knew we'd need and extra hug or two,
So he gave us friends,
So that we would always have an angel close when we needed one.

I never heard from this friend again, and could never trace him, so I assume it was a deathbed note, or he emigrated to avoid me.

Before you can make a success of life, in work as well as spiritually and socially, do you believe it is imperative to stick to the maxim 'Know thyself'?

Socrates' familiar view – that the unexamined life is not worth living – was probably inspired by the inscription 'Know thyself' at the shrine of the oracle of Delphi.

He saw in his fellow citizens of Athens a society that craved only money, power and fame, and was doomed to forever try to enlighten them.

Sadly, despite Socrates and the other great philosophers who followed him, society today appears indistinguishable from that of the Socratic era, except with knobs on.

So best not to do too much internalizing, particularly if like me, the view inside is not all that appealing.

Do you ever look up old school colleagues or attend school reunions, seek out friends from your young days, looking for them on Facebook, or on sites like Friends Reunited?

My youth is definitely Friends Disunited, and I don't know if that's because I'm too stuck here in the present, or too nervous about what I may dig up about my past.

Equally, people who knew me when I was young have been studiously effective at not seeking me out, and they must have their reasons.

Which is worse – a fib that saves a friend's feelings, or the truth that upsets them deeply?

I always feel that telling the truth and making someone cry is just as bad as telling a lie and making them smile.

But I've been called a 'phoney' so many times over the years, I've decided it's probably true.

As long as you accept that it's ok to be partially phoney, part of the time, I think this flaw applies to most people.

Or are you so hard-line in your position, that even a hint of phoniness, which slithers out occasionally, is wholly unforgivable?

You would have enjoyed the work of one of my heroes, Alan Sokal, a physics professor at New York University.

In 1996, Sokal submitted an article to *Social Text*, an academic journal of postmodern cultural studies. The thesis was an experiment to test the publication's intellectual rigour and, specifically, to learn if such a journal would "publish an article liberally salted with nonsense if it (a) sounded good and (b) flattered the editors' ideological preconceptions."

The article *"Transgressing the Boundaries: Towards a Transformative Hermeneutics of Quantum Gravity"*, proposed that quantum gravity is a social and linguistic construct.

At that time, the journal did not practice academic peer review and did not submit the article for outside expert analysis by a physicist.

On its date of publication, Sokal revealed that the article was a hoax, identifying it as "a pastiche of Left-wing cant, fawning references, grandiose statements, and outright nonsense... structured around the silliest quotations I could find about mathematics and physics".

The resultant academic and public quarrels concerned the scholarly merit, or lack thereof, of humanistic commentary about the physical sciences; the influence of postmodern philosophy on social disciplines in general; academic ethics, including whether Sokal was wrong to deceive the editors and readers of *Social Text*; and whether the journal had exercised the appropriate thoroughness before publishing the pseudoscientific article.

Alan Sokal is my kind of phoney, and something of a genius. And as they say: Talent hits a target no one else can hit; genius hits a target no one else can see.

As for phoniness in general, Oscar Levant understood it well. "Strip away the phoney tinsel of Hollwood, and you'll find the real tinsel underneath."

People tell me that my opinionated views show a lack of empathy with others, and a disregard for acceptable sensibilities.

But the truth is, although I believe almost everything I tell myself, I don't necessarily agree with everything I say.

Perhaps being rather insecure (vain and touchy) leads me to feel that whenever I have been invited to a party, it must be a party worth missing.

Someone once asked me if I had ever shaken hands with a member of the Royal Family and I was about to reply No, but thankfully remembered I had.

A wife and I were invited to dinner by Prince Charles (no gilt invitation, his office rang), and I thought it might be entertaining, just the four of us at Windsor Castle.

Or perhaps, they would have another couple over as well?

The line to shake our host's hand stretched back 50 yards, and of course I was ready to bolt for it, but like a starstruck fool, hung on.

He seemed pleased to be introduced, and I soon learned why I had made it onto the invitation list. 'I have a small collection of my watercolours that I spent the Summer on, just through there, do let me know what you think.' I started looking at the watercolours in a magnificent large room at 7.30pm, with 380 of his other close friends.

Nobody was allowed into the grand dining hall until 8.30pm, so we all had plenty of time to admire each delightful sketch. At the allotted hour, we stood at our designated placements waiting for Prince Charles to be seated, before anyone else could be. A small choir sang a charming musical tribute to the Royal Family.

I discovered that I was positioned next to Geri Halliwell. I can't be doing with 1990s Britpop, so I had no idea at the time who she was, but found her quick, funny and bright, and if you like gingers, not bad looking at all. The table was so wide the people opposite were hard to see, let alone talk to, but on my other side was a delightful lady with a diamond on her ring the size of a decent conker.

The food was memorable. Tiny fragments of nouvelle cuisine, everything tastefully decorated with crossed chives. I obviously stopped at McDonalds, Wandsworth on the way home.

I just opened another corker of an invite. It reads:

You plus three companions are invited to visit the Roden Crater art project in the Arizona desert, still being completed, yet even now very beautiful, and claimed one day to be the American Sistine Chapel. The artist behind the project is James Turrell, known for using light in art.

The trip would leave London Heathrow on the afternoon of the 11th of November 2011, flying British Airways First Class to Phoenix, then by private jet to Flagstaff, Arizona. There will then be a two nights stay at the beautifully located Little America Hotel in Flagstaff.

On the afternoon of the 12th of November, you will be taken on the trip to Roden Crater; it will take around one hour to reach Roden Crater from the hotel. The tour of the crater will last around three hours, with a light meal at the end. Without a doubt the best time to view Roden Crater is around sunset, hence the afternoon visit.

After a relaxing Sunday morning, you will be taken in the afternoon by private jet from Flagstaff to Phoenix, from there by British Airways First Class back to London Heathrow, arriving early afternoon on the 14th of November.

The total cost of the trip, covering yourself and three companions, plus myself who will escort you, will be £146,989. This will include a donation of £51,000 to the on-going Roden Crater project, which may one day be the ultimate work of art.

If you feel you may be interested in the above, please contact myself, Paul Gee on 07535 059 236.

I'm sure you could be invited if you would care to follow up on Mr Gee's enticing offer.

I often dread having a dinner party host show me his collection of art. Ambassador Richard Washburn Child once dined with Calvin Coolidge at the White House.

After dinner, the President said he had something to show him. He led Child to one of the smaller rooms in the mansion, opened the door, and turned on the light.

"On the opposite wall hung a portrait of himself," Child later recalled. "I thought it so very bad I could think of nothing to say." For a long moment the two men stood on the threshold.

Then Coolidge snapped off the light and closed the door. "So do I," he said.

Jane Eyre engraving by Joseph Karl Stieler, 1781-1858

DO YOU HAVE A TOILET FACE?

It may sound insulting, but it isn't at all. It doesn't question your handsomeness, or your beauty, or whether you are simply downright plain.

If you have a toilet face, you appear to others as open and engaging – a countenance that strangers would approach on the street when seeking directions to the nearest lavatory.

Some people may look strikingly attractive, but not to someone requiring pressing assistance.

Jane Eyre, perhaps our most treasured plain-looking girl, would have been ideally suited to this task – neither too daunting to be selected for your enquiry, nor too indecisive-looking to be of much help, but someone who seems approachable and guileless, unreserved and straightforward.

In general however, people who are pleasing to look at have a better time of it – and that has eternally been the case. Aristotle probably wasn't the first to point out that beauty is a greater recommendation than any letter of introduction.

Did you ever read a novel called *Uglies*, published in 2005?

Neither did I, but apparently the premise was that in a future dystopian world, everybody is automatically given a cosmetic surgery makeover upon reaching the age of sixteen.

I imagine it was aimed at young adults, as the main protagonist, Tally Youngblood, doesn't hold with this enforced conformity, and tries to encourage her teenage friends that they don't need to become 'Pretties' – because it transpires that part of the transformation includes brain implants to ensure inhabitants are placid, or 'pretty minded'.

Frankly, it all sounds like a rather serene and pleasant life, surrounded by nobody other than deeply appealing people.

But being a beauty can have its downsides, apparently.

According to the University of Colorado Business School, attractive women are discriminated against in roles such as Manager of Research and Development, Director of Finance, etc.

In 'masculine' careers, according to Professor Johnson, 'being attractive is highly detrimental to women, whereas attractive men suffer no similar discrimination.'

Good-looking women were sought after for positions like receptionists or secretaries, but as the study concludes, researchers found that the 'beauty is beastly' effect hinders women seeking employment in a number of male-oriented jobs.

People can be quite capable of deciding whether they would be better off joining BeautifulPeople.com as an online dating matchmaking service, or TheUglyBugBall.com.

At BeautifulPeople.com you face having your application rejected if you are not considered appealing enough.

'We have to follow our founding principles of only accepting beautiful people – that's what our members have paid for,' they explain.

And they can be brutally harsh in their assessments.

Only 9% of male Irish applicants were accepted, and only 20% of Irish women, compared to 70% of Swedish women who signed up.

Brazilian and Scandinavian men have the greatest chance of being accepted to the exclusive listings of 700,000 around the world.

In the desire for facial enhancement, hundreds of billions are spent globally on beauty treatments of all kinds.

And before you criticise people who attempt to Botox their way to beauty, a study reported in *Psychology Today* is intriguing.

Dermatological specialist Dr Eric Finzi evaluated the effectiveness of Botox in treating depression. After a nine month course, patients with depression or even bi-polar disorders were reported to have clinically supported evidence of recovery.

Stanford University psychologist Robert Zajonc suggests the effect may be due to relaxed facial muscles cooling the blood flowing to the brain in much the same way as the relaxing disciplines of Yoga or Tai Chi.

Before you rush off to be Botoxed all over in the hope of becoming a really cheery person, there is no large-scale support for these views amongst leading medical experts.

Over at TheUglyBugBall.com they specialise in 'real dating for real people'. In their 'welcome to reality code', they offer 'five ugly truths about meeting others':

1. Half of daters aren't pretty, so instead of fishing in a small pool of prettiness and getting nowhere, dive into an ocean of uglies and have more choice.
2. Ugly people are a better calibre of human – pretty people generally aren't very nice and tend to be a bit shallow.
3. Ugly people have had a tougher life and therefore tend to be more considerate and more loyal. Our survey also proved that they try harder in bed.
4. Once with an ugly partner, it is unlikely that anyone will try and take them from you, meaning you can let yourself go completely once you're together.
5. In these straightened times our service is cheaper as a) We don't charge as much as the pretty sites and b) Ugly people have lower expectations – for a first date a Family Bucket will usually do the trick.

Finally they point out: 'If you are one of the millions of people that don't always like what they see in the mirror, then this is the place for you.'

And if you are plain enough to be truly interesting, there is a career path waiting for you at Ugly Models, with their roster of 1,000 less-than-conventionally-pretty people.

Their models are in great demand as character roles in a variety of films and photographs, everything from James Bond to Marks & Spencer, from Calvin Klein advertisements to Italian Vogue, to Harry Potter movies.

'We had a very overweight lady,' explains the Ugly agency, 'who was unhappy with herself, but since she's been taking roles as a big person, she is loving being larger than life.'

Of course there is a difference between being so plain that you are a 'character' and being just pleasant-looking enough to make other people feel at ease and comfortable around you.

There you have it. No need to be gorgeous. With a toilet face, you have just the countenance that attracts incontinence.

Note: At the Sulabh Museum of Toilets in New Delhi, India,
visitors can follow the evolution of the lavatory in various
cultures around the world.

A woodcut of one of Jack the Ripper's victims

ISN'T EVERYBODY SCHIZOPHRENIC, OR IS IT JUST ME?

Allow me to introduce myselves.

On days when I am dangerously under-medicated, nine out of ten voices in my head tell me I am sane.

You, too, can probably tell when you are behaving like a booby, and part of you knows that you can't stick your foot into a closed mouth, and another part warns you that if something goes without saying, let it.

It doesn't mean we are not wholly competent. But if you are a bit cack-handed like me, you do begin to believe that we are living testimony that for every idiot-proof system devised, a new, improved idiot will arise and overcome it.

So of course, I can still only use a vintage Nokia, no 3G, no camera, no apps, nothing to baffle or belittle me. Quite simple people can apparently master the manifold functions of the latest smartphone; this only goes to confound me further.

But I have a challenge to all of you technologically alert types: while sitting at your desk, lift your right foot off the floor and make clockwise circles. Now, while doing this draw the number '6' in the air with your right hand. Your foot will change direction and there's nothing you can do about it.

Somehow, believe it or not, I can manage to do it…

Of course there are some things that nobody has the answers to. Why do men have nipples for example? Some theorists think men should be able to produce milk, on the basis that everyone is born with mammary glands, but so far history has failed to produce such a man.

It appears nature can be capricious, and just decided that nipples should be imprinted on everyone's DNA blueprint, amongst other useless bits of apparatus like appendices and wisdom teeth.

And nobody knows the secret formula for manufacturing Coca-Cola. Except for two people on earth, that is.

The original copy of the formula is kept in the SunTrust Bank in Atlanta. To be sure the bank would always ensure the secret was kept safe, Coke gave them 48.3 million shares of stock, as well as having executives from each company sit on each other's board of directors.

Only two Coke executives at any time are allowed to be privy to the formula. It is so fiercely protected that the company even pulled out of India in the 1970s because they would have been legally required to divulge their ingredient list to their government. When one of the Coke heirs ended his marriage to his wife, and she demanded some of his great-grandfather's (the founder of Coca-Cola) original notes as part of her settlement, the Company took over the divorce proceedings and settlement out of fear the notes could contain information on the formula.

Coca-Cola has one other form of protection. It is the only company in the US to have government permission to import the coca plant legally. So even if you had the formula, you wouldn't be able to copy the Coke taste without the coca plant; if you then decided to import the coca plant illegally, it would be more profitable to use it as its most lucrative resource in the manufacture of cocaine.

Another secret yet to be unearthed is the true identity of Jack the Ripper. Nor has anyone found Jack the Stripper, come to that.

I don't have any theories, any more than the police do about Jack the Stripper, an unknown serial killer responsible for the London 'Nude Murders' between 1964 and 1965.

His victimology and nickname were similar to the more famous Jack. He murdered six, possibly eight prostitutes, all under 30 years old, whose naked bodies were discovered around London or dumped in the River Thames. Chief Superintendent John Du Rose of Scotland Yard interviewed 7,000 suspects. He then held a number of news conferences, announcing the suspect pool had narrowed to 10, and then to 3.

Jack the Stripper was never found, but at least the murders stopped after the initial press conference. John Du Rose wrote his autobiography *Murder Was My Business* in 1973, if you would care to read about his most grisly cases.

I have finally uncovered the mystery someone once asked me about – why if there are twenty people in a room, there's a 50/50 chance that two of them will have the same birthday.

This phenomenon actually has a name – it is called the Birthday Paradox – and the reason it is so surprising is because we know it is most unlikely that anyone we meet will share the same birthday.

For example, if you meet someone randomly, the chance of your sharing the same date is only 1/365. Even if you ask 20 people, the probability is still low – less than 5%. When you put 20 people in a room however, the key change is that each of the 20 people is now asking each of the other 19 people about their birthdays. Each individual person only has a small chance of a success, but each person is trying it 19 times. That increases the probability dramatically.

Because my maths was always particularly weak, and has now solidified with rust, I thought I would ask a mathematics specialist to explain this in a way that was crystal clear. His reply was: 364/365 * 363/365 * … 365-20+1/365 = Chances of no collisions.

I hope that clarifies it for you.

For me, it's time to repress another memory. Particularly the one when my parents tell me I am one of those bad things that happen to good people.

In any event, schizophrenia beats dining alone.

An expert on such a matter was Jorge Beltrao Negromonte da Silveira, author of *Revelations of a Schizophrenic*.

He was also one of the participants in a religious sect in Brazil that killed and ate at least three women as part of their rituals.

When the cannibals confessed to the crime, they explained that a voice had told them to kill evil females, and to stuff the leftover meat into empanadas, which they then sold on to their unwitting neighbours.

Joconde pardon Mallet, 1883, etching by Jean De La Fontaine

LOVE MEANS FOREVER HAVING TO SAY YOU'RE SORRY.

Are you good at apologising? Unlike most men, I'm very good, and alarmingly plausible, however insincere. If you can practise apologising until you become utterly convincing, everyone's happy.

You, because you have made life more harmonious with minimum effort; and the recipient of the apology, because he – or she – feels vindicated and superior.

There is absolutely no shame in a good apology, deftly made; even with your fingers crossed behind your back, it can generally be quite elevating.

Psychology Today's Dr. Sam Margulies is a mediation specialist and considered the master of apology management. He believes men and women regard apologies from very different perspectives.

For women, apologising is a way of reconnecting with someone whose feelings you have hurt, however inadvertently.

When a woman is told that something she has or hasn't done has offended or upset someone, she is usually quick to apologise, thereby avoiding a breach in the relationship and allowing it to continue undisturbed. Whether she is offering an apology or receiving one, a woman will tend to regard it as an important part of making her relationships work.

Men are very different. Men tend to see apologies as somehow belittling – at some level, an apology involves a loss of face. Scholars of gender relations have observed that for men, verbal communication is tied up with concern for the way their status is regarded by others.

Men are far more conscious of how the things they say affect others peoples' perceptions of their power – or lack of power. For a man, acknowledging that he has done something wrong often leads to him feeling diminished in the eyes of those who hear the apology. He feels a sense of loss – even humiliation – and as a result, he is reluctant to apologise. In many cases, he does not even know *how* to craft a sincere apology.

It seems that in most modern marriages it is more often the case that the woman is angry at her husband, rather than the other way round. Women express anger at their husband's sins of commission as well as sins of omission. And the most common sin of omission is his failure to say sorry when he has offended.

So, with that in mind, here is a brief tutorial.

The necessary elements of an apology for a gentleman:

There are six elements of a proper apology. If you do not want to waste your time you must include all six.

1. **Acknowledge the wrongful act**
   Begin by saying, 'I was wrong and I am sorry.' There are no substitutes for this admission. If you say something silly like, 'I am sorry you think I was wrong', you might as well not bother. There is no getting around it. You were wrong, so plead guilty and get on with it.

2. **Acknowledge that you have hurt her feelings**
   Understand that your wrongful act has hurt her feelings and made her feel disconnected from you. You won't be able to reconnect without first attending to her pain. Say, 'I was wrong and I am sorry that I have hurt your feelings.' Once again, there is no substitute: you cannot fudge the issue by saying, 'I am sorry that you're upset.' You have to connect your wrongful act to her hurt feelings.

3. **Express remorse**
   An expression of remorse and regret is the way you demonstrate your ability to feel an appropriate response to her hurt feelings. Say, 'I was wrong and I am sorry that I hurt your feelings and I feel terrible that I have done something that has hurt you.' (It will help here if you actually look remorseful.)

4. **State your intention not to repeat offend**
   This may be difficult, particularly if you are indeed a repeat offender, but it is an expression of your acknowledgement of your need to reform. 'I know that I can be insensitive to your needs but I am going to try my hardest not to do it again.' Smirk at

this juncture and your apology will collapse; you'll be back at square one and have to start over.

5. Offer to make amends

If you don't know what would help, ask. 'What can I do to make it up to you?' The particular act of contrition may be negotiated, but the important thing is to express your willingness to do something by way of compensation. Of course, once you commit to that something, you need to do it – or you render the entire effort useless.

6. Seek forgiveness

Forgiving is an act that liberates the forgiver from their own anger, so seeking forgiveness is not as self-serving as you may think. A simple, 'Will you forgive me?' will usually suffice, but if you want to avoid appearing presumptuous, or if your offense was particularly odious, you might first ask, 'Can you forgive me?'

As you get better at it you will feel more comfortable creating your own set of 'rules' for making apologies, and adding touches here and there that individualise your efforts.

But always remember there is a simple way of destroying any apology - using the word 'if'. For example, 'I am sorry if I hurt you,' or 'I'm sorry if that came across wrong'.

Remember instead to always use the 'that' word, as in 'I am sorry that I hurt you, and that it came across wrong'.

Did you know about I'mSorry.com?

It's a website apology community offering people the ability to apologise online, share apology stories and send forgive-me gifts and cards.

They tell visitors "We developed I'm Sorry to help make the world a better place. If people hurt others in a deliberate or unintentional way, we wish to make it easier to make amends. So for every six dollars you spend on an 'I'm Sorry Card' we distribute two dollars to approved charities around the world to feed hungry children. Make the world a better place, one apology at a time!"

What a charming notion, and probably better than my own code of conduct: An apology is a good way to have the last word.

'The pen is mightier than the sword' was written by English author Edward Bulwer-Lytton in 1839 for his play *Richelieu*, seen here, though versions of this phrase have appeared since the Assyrian sage Ahiqar used it in about 500 BC. Sadly, he has been disproved countless times since.

THE SWORD IS MIGHTIER THAN THE PEN.

On the United Nations website, pages are devoted to its role in freeing the world from the possibility of war.

However utopian this view, and however helpful the UN's soothing words have been in allaying conflict, after the United Nations' charter was ratified in 1945, its collective pen has had no effect in preventing the 186 wars that have since taken place around the world.

The written word is clearly a less forceful tool than a rocket launcher and an assault rifle.

However, after frittering away my best years writing advertising copy, I obviously believe in the power of words and imagery – and it's easy to demonstrate. Faced with just the names of well known celebrities, people conjure up vivid, wildly varying impressions of each person.

If I say "Bono" for example, many of you will see a titan of modern music, a wonderful showman whose performances fill the heart, a beacon of goodness, using his fame to promote charity and conscience. Others would say "Bono" is a dull singer of corny songs, whose acclaim is mystifying, and whose "charedy" work is a crutch to inflate his own sense of self-importance.

We form strong opinions about people we have never met, but seen and heard a great deal about through words and pictures that have shaped and influenced us.

Another example, "Paris Hilton" some would find sparkly and fresh, her immense charm resting in her ability to hide her light behind a dotty, air-headed persona, even though her IQ is probably in the high 160's.

Others would say "Paris Hilton" is rather plain, quite stupid and utterly talentless – another of those bizarre people who have emerged in the last decade who are famous for their famousness.

My point here is that some people are swayed by pictures, some people are persuaded by words: it is the structure of our brain cells which determines whether we prefer one over the other, or both equally. Or neither – some people just like country walks.

Of course motivations for conflict, whether they be Hitler's *Lebensraum*, or religious differences, ethnic divides or the simple madness and greed of sociopath dictators, are difficult to deflect even with the most lucid diplomacy.

In political propaganda, a decent set of slogans, speeches and soundbites are of little help against a candidate who is captivating on television; a candidate who's magnetism tasers voters into submission, despite a woolly campaign.

Everybody in advertising had heard talk of the "Golden Chalice of Subliminal Advertising". I can safely say I have never seen an example, though people tell me of tests in America in the 1950's where they flashed super quick images of an icy Coca-Cola onto the screen, apparently invisible to the eye, and saw sales of Coke in the cinema triple immediately.

Of course, it could be that they also turned off the air conditioning when the tests took place in Arizona in midsummer, to help pull off this master-stroke.

Subliminal advertising is an urban myth, and nowhere near as much fun as a commercial that makes you laugh, or think. That's not to say I wouldn't much prefer subliminal versions of the endless Churchill, Go Compare, Confused.com commercials that air pitilessly.

I still remember the little homily passed down to generations of advertising copywriters since the 1930's.
"When the client moans and sighs, make his logo twice the size.
Should this still be unsatisfactory, show a picture of his factory.
Only in the direst case, show a picture of his face".

I had fewer of my advertising ideas rejected by clients as I got older, and my ideas got duller. The Inland Revenue, for some reason didn't like the slogan 'We've got what it takes to take what you've got.'

I thought it rather charming, and crucially, highly believable.

The power of words to convey a message is easiest in English, supposedly the most dense of all languages, drawing on an immense vocabulary to enable broader descriptions of every object or emotion.

But there are a number of foreign words that simply don't have an equivalent in English. How would you translate the Russian word 'Toska', for example?

Vladmir Nabokov describes it best:
'No single word in English renders all the shades of toska. At its deepest and most painful, it is a sensation of great spiritual anguish, often without any specific cause.

At less morbid levels it is a dull ache of the soul, a longing with nothing to long for, a sick pining, a vague restlessness, mental throes, yearning. In particular cases, it may be the desire for somebody of something specific, nostalgia, love-sickness. At the lowest level it grades into ennui, boredom.'

2. Litost (Czech)
The state of agony and torment that comes from a sudden comprehension of one's own misery.

3. Ya'aburnee (Arabic)
The literal translation is, 'You bury me' which is simultaneously gruesome and romantic. It conveys the speaker's hope that he should die before a beloved other – his fear that if the other were the first to die, he could not go on living.

4. Duende (Spanish)
Originally the word to describe a mythical pixie-like creature with the power to possess human beings and cause them to feel overawed by their natural habitat. The meaning has now shifted and refers to the way that a

work of art can affect people in mysterious, powerful and profoundly moving ways.

5. Saudade (Portuguese)
One of the most saddest words and famously difficult to translate, the idea of saudade is steeped in tradition and is communicated in Fado music. It captures a feeling of melancholia and heartfelt longing for the loss of something or someone.

6. Jayus (Indonesian)
A really poor joke, badly told, and so unfunny you have to laugh.

7. Iktsuarpok (Inuit)
To venture outside to see if anyone might be coming.

8. Cafune (Brazilian Portuguese)
Encapsulates the tender act of running one's fingers through another person's hair.

9. Dépaysement (French)
The feeling of being away from one's country – a kind of national rather than domestic homesickness.

10. Hyggelig (Danish)
Connotes the cosiness and warmth felt when one is in happy surroundings among family and close friends.

11. Tartle (Scottish)
The moment of hesitation when you have to introduce someone and you realize you can't remember their name.

However potent language may be at stirring emotions, sadly mankind is still often at the mercy of a well-armed despot, uninterested in turning swords into ploughshares, or indeed pens.

Let Us Beat Swords into Ploughshares,
a sculpture by Evgeniy Vuchetich, given by the
Soviet Union to the United Nations in 1959

Acknowledgements

First published in 2013 by
Booth-Clibborn Editions
www.booth-clibborn.com
Text © 2013 Charles Saatchi
Printed and bound in China
ISBN 978-1-86154-337-0

Edited and designed by Georgina Marling
Author photograph by James King

Image credits
82 - Photograph by Yousuf Karsh,
Camera Press London
188 - Photo by Carlo Bavagnoli/Time Life
Pictures/Getty Images

Booth-Clibborn Editions has made all
reasonable efforts to reach artists, photographers
and/or copyright owners of images used in this
book. We are prepared to pay fair and
reasonable fees for any usage made without
compensation agreement.

The information in this book is based on
material supplied to Booth-Clibborn
Editions/Abrams by the author. While every
effort has been made to ensure accuracy, Booth-
Clibborn Editions does not under any
circumstances accept responsibility for any
errors or omissions.

A Cataloguing-in-Publication record for this
book is available from the Publisher.

Booth-Clibborn Editions
Studio 83,
235 Earls Court Road,
London SW5 OEB

Distributed by Abrams/Chronicle books
www.abramsbooks.com
The Market Building,
72-74 Rosebery Avenue,
London EC1R 4RW

The author wishes to thank a number of
websites and other source material that have
helped with research, used verbatim where their
clarity cannot be improved.

www.bbc.co.uk
www.blastr.com
www.cracked.com - Jacopo Della Quercia
www.cracked.com - Marc Russel
www.dailydawdle.com
www.didyouknowarchive.com
www.disinfo.com
www.dizzy-dee.com
www.extremescience.com
www.futilitycloset.com
www.gizmodo.com - Brent Rose
www.helpguide.org
www.howstuffworks.com
www.huffingtonpost.com
www.imgdumpr.com
www.listverse.com
www.mentalfloss.com
www.misconceptionjunction.com
www.news.discovery.com
www.null-hypothesis.co.uk
www.odditycentral.com
www.parents.berkeley.edu
www.ponderabout.com
www.psychologytoday.com - Gretchen Rubin
www.psychologytoday.com - Dr. Sam Margulies
www.quora.com
www.rawfoodinfo.com
www.secret-london.co.uk
www.seedmagazine.com - Joe Kloc
www.stevecarter.com
www.tastefullyoffensive.com
www.thescavenger.net - Erin Stewart
www.theweek.com
www.theworldgeography.com
www.thinkorthwim.com
www.toptenz.net
www.travelever.com
www.twistedsifter.com
www.wikipedia.org
www.wordnik.com
www.wordorigins.org